NEW TESTAMENT
EVERYDAY BIBLE STUDIES

EPHESIANS
AND
COLOSSIANS

DIVERSITY IN UNITY

SCOT MCKNIGHT

QUESTIONS WRITTEN BY
BECKY CASTLE MILLER

HarperChr
Resources

T0407151

New Testament Everyday Bible Study Series: Ephesians and Colossians
© 2025 by Scot McKnight

Published in Grand Rapids, Michigan, by HarperChristian Resources.
HarperChristian Resources is a registered trademark of HarperCollins
Christian Publishing, Inc.

Requests for information should be sent to customercare@harpercollins.com.

ISBN 978-0-310-12947-9 (softcover)
ISBN 978-0-310-12948-6 (ebook)

HarperChristian Resources titles may be purchased in bulk for church,
business, fundraising, or ministry use. For information, please e-mail
ResourceSpecialist@ChurchSource.com.

First Printing April 2025 / Printed in the United States of America

For the DMin and DTM students of 2025

CONTENTS

COLOSSIANS

GENERAL INTRODUCTION

Christians make a claim for the Bible not made of any other book. Or, since the Bible is a library shelf of many authors, it's a claim we make of no other shelf of books. We claim that God worked in each of the authors as they were writing so that what was scratched on papyrus expressed what God wanted communicated to the people of God. Which makes the New Testament (NT) a book unlike any other book. Which is why Christians are reading the NT almost two thousand years later with great delight. These books have the power to instruct us and to rebuke us and to correct us and to train us to walk with God every day. We read these books because God speaks to us in them.

Developing a routine of reading the Bible with an open heart, a receptive mind, and a flexible will is the "why" of the *New Testament Everyday Bible Studies*. But not every day will be the same. Some days we pause and take it in, and other days we stop and repent and lament and open ourselves to God's restoring graces. No one word suffices for what the Bible does to us. In fact, the Bible's own view of the Bible can be found by reading Psalm 119, the longest chapter in the Bible with 176 verses! It is a meditation on eight terms for what the Bible is and what the Bible does to those who listen and read it. Its laws instruct us and order us, its statutes direct us, its precepts inform us, its decrees guide us, its commands compel us, its words speak to us, and its promises comfort us, and it is no wonder that the author can sum all eight up as the "way" (119:3). Each of those terms still speaks to what happens when we open our minds to the Word of God.

Every day with the Bible then is new because our timeless and timely God communes with us in our daily lives in our world and in our time. Just as God spoke to Jesus in Galilee and Paul in Ephesus and John on Patmos. These various contexts help us hear God in our context so the New Testament Everyday Bible Studies will often delve into contexts. Most of us now have a Bible on our devices. We may well have several translations available to us everywhere we go every day. To hear those words, we are summoned by God to open the Bible, to attune our hearts to God, and to listen to what God says. My prayer is that these daily study guides will help each of us become daily Bible readers attentive to the mind of God.

INTRODUCTION: READING PAUL'S LETTERS TO THE EPHESIANS AND COLOSSIANS

These two letters belong together, not only because they were written toward the end of the apostle Paul's life but also because their themes connect. The letters urge two churches in Western Asia Minor to stay faithful to the teachings about Christ and about the church. They also advocate unity among all believers in Jesus Christ, with Ephesians emphasizing grace and Colossians growth, though each teaches both of those ideas.

Ephesus is today one of the world's greatest archaeological sites while Colossae, just a short drive away from Ephesus, has not yet been subjected to an extensive "dig." Soon, we hope. Paul moved the center of his mission work from Antioch to Ephesus in the second half of his mission, and from there he and his team of workers planted churches in Western Asia Minor and in Greece. Perhaps because Ephesus was so central to his ministry, and because he had spent so much of his time there along with those closest to himself, the letter to the Ephesians has a quality unlike any other letter of Paul's (and his co-authors). In fact, "To God's holy people" may not have originally even had "in Ephesus." This letter may well represent the theological vision of Paul for the churches in his orbit. Ephesians appears to be a circular letter. Perhaps centered in Ephesus, the letter may have been sent to others of Paul's churches.

Like Colossians, the letter begins in prayer with sublime heights and presses home the importance of unity. The admonition, "Make every effort to keep the unity of the Spirit" speaks to the peace-bond that the Spirit and grace generate in churches marked off with one body, one Spirit, one hope, one Lord, one faith, one baptism, and one God and Father of all (Ephesians 4:3–6). Grace does not show up in these various unifying features, but it is under them all, appearing a beautiful dozen times along with other cognates like forgiveness, which can be translated as "gracing." We approach unity in Ephesians with the theme of grace, and in Colossians with the theme of growth. If grace is under all the unities, being "in Christ" locates the unities, and this expression occurs more than a dozen times (e.g., 1:1, 3, 9, 12, 13—and that's just the first chapter). The same expression occurs seven times in Colossians.

Ephesians has a generic feel, a summary feel, even a sense that the message sums up Paul's instructions for a number of churches. Colossians has a local feel, and co-authors, Paul and Timothy point out the church planter whom they guided. His name was Epaphras, and our two authors admired his spiritual and pastoral life (Colossians 1:7–8; 4:12–13). What stands out as local in Colossians is the problematic people and their ideas. One quick reading, however, will never grasp the complicated nature of what these people were teaching (cf. 2:8–23). The problems are intense enough that many think the entire letter's emphasis on

Christology, growth, and the gospel are shaped to respond to those problems. Thus, the beautiful song-like words of 1:15–20 probably do set the stage for affirming that all of God's fullness is to be found in Christ (1:19; 2:9–10). As God's fullness, living in Christ is entirely sufficient for all the Colossians' needs (2:6–7, 8, 9–15).

Of all Paul's letters these two have the most tendencies to become abstract. Yet, for all that abstraction, the practicalities of living the Christian life in Western Asia Minor bleed through the prose in every section. For Ephesians, notice 1:13–14; 2:8–10; 4:1–16, and then especially 4:17–6:20. For Colossians, take note of 1:10–14, 21–23; 2:6–7, 13–15, and then especially 3:1–4:6.

At the center of these two letters, as well as at the center of Paul's own life and all his letters and ministry, was Jesus Christ. In these two letters you will come to see that Jesus is Creator, Redeemer, and Sustainer of all creation. In him the fullness of God lives bodily, and he is all the believers needed then and need now. The letters urge us to keep our eyes on Jesus Christ.

WORKS CITED IN THE STUDY GUIDE

(Throughout the Guide you will find the author's name and title in brackets, as noted in this book listing, with page numbers whenever I cite something from it):

Ephesians

First Nations Version: An Indigenous Translation of the New Testament (Downers Grove: IVP, 2021). [*First Nations*]
Lynn H. Cohick, *The Letter to the Ephesians* (Grand

Rapids: Wm. B. Eerdmans, 2020). [Cohick, *Ephesians*]

Lynn. H. Cohick, *Ephesians*, Proclamation: Preaching the New Testament (Eugene, Oregon: Cascade, 2024). [Cohick, Proclamation]

Esau D. McCaulley, "Letter to the Ephesians," in Esau McCaulley, et al., *The New Testament in Color: A Multiethnic Bible Commentary* (Downers Grove: IVP Academic, 2024),414–438. [McCaulley, "Ephesians"]

Scot McKnight, *The Second Testament: A New Translation* (Downers Grove: IVP Academic, 2023). [McKnight, *Second Testament*]

Claire M. Powell, "Ephesians," in *The Women's Bible Commentary*, ed. Catherine Clark Kroeger, Mary J. Evans (Downers Grove: IVP, 2002), 694–706.

Mark D. Roberts, *Ephesians* (Grand Rapids: Zondervan, 2016). [Roberts, *Ephesians*]

Mitzi J. Smith, "Ephesians," in *True to Our Native Land: An African American New Testament Commentary*, Second Edition (Minneapolis: Fortress, 2007, 2024), 369–384. [Smith, "Ephesians—2 ed."]

Colossians

First Nations Version: An Indigenous Translation of the New Testament (Downers Grove: IVP, 2021). [*First Nations*]

Shirley A. Decker-Lucke, "Colossians," in *The IVP Women's Bible Commentary*, ed. Catherine Clark Kroeger, Mary J. Evans (Downers Grove: IVP, 2002), 714–721. [Decker-Lucke, "Colossians"]

Dennis R. Edwards, "Letter to the Colossians," in Esau

McCaulley, et al., *The New Testament in Color: A Multiethnic Bible Commentary* (Downers Grove: IVP Academic, 2024),414–438. [D. Edwards, "Colossians"]

Margaret Y. MacDonald, *Colossians and Ephesians*, Sacra Pagina 17 (Collegeville, Minnesota: Liturgical Press, 2008). [MacDonald, *Colossians*]

Scot McKnight, *The Letter to the Colossians*, New International Commentary on the New Testament (Grand Rapids: Wm. B. Eerdmans, 2018). [McKnight, *Colossians*]. Throughout this Everyday Bible Study, I have assumed my own work, but I will not cite it unless I am quoting it.

David W. Pao, *Colossians and Philemon*, Zondervan Exegetical Commentary on the New Testament (Grand Rapids: Zondervan, 2012). [Pao, *Colossians*]

EPHESIANS

GOOD THINGS ABOUT THE GOD OF GRACE

Ephesians 1:1–10

[1] *Paul, an apostle of Christ Jesus by the will of God,*

To God's holy people in Ephesus, the faithful in Christ Jesus:

[2] ***Grace** and peace to you from God our Father and the Lord Jesus Christ.*

[3] *Praise be to the God and Father of our Lord Jesus Christ, who has <u>blessed</u> us in the heavenly realms with <u>every spiritual blessing</u> in Christ. [4] For he <u>chose</u> us in him before the creation of the world to be holy and blameless in his sight. In **love** [5] he <u>predestined</u> us for <u>adoption to sonship</u> through Jesus Christ, in accordance with his pleasure and will—[6] to the praise of his glorious **grace**, which he has **freely given** us in the One he loves. [7] In him we have <u>redemption</u> through his blood, <u>the forgiveness of sins</u>, in accordance with the riches of God's **grace** [8] that he lavished on us. With all wisdom and understanding, [9] he made known to us the <u>mystery</u> of his will according to his good pleasure, which he purposed in Christ, [10] to be put into effect when the times reach their fulfillment—to bring <u>unity</u> to all things in heaven and on earth under Christ.*

Paul has so many good things to say about God that he can't help writing a sentence in which one word after another tumbles out of his mouth. What tumbles out are both God's acts (*italics*) and supporting words about God's acts (<u>underlined</u>), which are all done out of God's gracious love (**bold**). We learn in this passage that God, well before creation, loved us and, because of that love, directed his grace toward humans. Grace expresses love. Love is first. So now, please read the passage pausing over each term marked in italics, underlined, and bolded. "The overarching message of this passage is God's blessing of salvation, enacted in Christ and sealed with the Holy Spirit" (Cohick, Proclamation, 10). No passage in the Bible more densely narrates the story of God and our place in God's story.

To be sure, Paul opens the letter as he does other letters: naming himself and his calling ("apostle") and his audience. A friend, A.J. Swoboda, a pastor and professor, mentioned to me in an email a fresh approach to understanding what Paul meant by apostle of Christ Jesus. Swoboda explained, "he had to say that at the beginning of his letters to remind himself of who he was. When you spend your life and ministry being beaten up, you have to have an internal sense of clarity as to the person you are—and the calling God has given to you. Many pastors need to be reminded of their calling. And in so doing, they can put up with the people throwing darts their way" (Swoboda, email, 6 August 2024). This surely resonates with the Paul I have come to love and know. He knew who and whose he was, and that gave him the courage to face whatever came his way.

Not one word in today's central passage (vv. 3–10) describes what we need to do in order to experience this blessing. We wait for verse twelve for that, and at that point Paul says that we are those who "put our hope in Christ."

One verse later he adds *believing* to hope. Knowing what's ahead permits us to detect an echo of this faith-based hope in verse one's "the faithful in Christ Jesus."

Paul's first word, translated in the NIV with "Praise" comes from the Greek word *eulogētos*, from which we get our word eulogy. Lynn Cohick, in fact, calls this section a "eulogy" (Cohick, *Ephesians*, 83). The term means "to say good words," and that's exactly what Paul does in today's (and tomorrow's) reading. Though we use the term eulogy mostly about someone who has recently died, we can learn a lesson from Paul here—we can eulogize God, and others (living or in the hands of God), for their character, attributes, gifts, and actions. Actually, Paul learned this way of eulogizing God in his scriptures and synagogue (cf. 1 Kings 8:15, 56; Psalm 72:18–19; Luke 1:68–79). At the heart of Paul's good words about God are (1) God's redemptive work, (2) in Christ, and (3) for *all* people. "Too often the majority culture church in America has treated itself as the center of God's purposes," but the witness of Paul's gospel of grace is the elevation of all people into the people of God (McCaulley, "Ephesians," 417). All of this occurs in Christ, so we can claim that to the degree we are not united with all others in Christ, we are not truly living "in" Christ. We may well discover we have one foot outside that "in Christ" circle.

One of the privileges of my career is traveling to speak, and no place has been more enjoyable than Denmark. A few times I have spoken at their Sommer Oase event in Odder, not too far south from Aarhus. Kris and I are not up on the latest Christian songs, so we were in for a real treat when the first evening at Oase a local worship team led us in worship, singing a song with the words "hosanna" and "in the highest." It was magical, it drew us into the worship, and we were lifted into the heavenlies. We knew enough German (yes) to see what the probable Danish words were. But, as we have all learned, good music takes good words to a higher level. We did not know they were singing an Australian song called "Hosanna in the Highest," which everyone around us seemed to know in both Danish and English. Wherever they learned that song, we knew the Danes knew what it meant to join Paul in saying good things about God.

Before we get started, I call your attention to an oddity about this letter. Some of the earliest and most reliable manuscripts of this letter do not have "in Ephesus." If the original did not have "in Ephesus," it was because the letter, perhaps written from Ephesus, was intended to be sent to several churches. Thus, it would have been a circular letter. We cannot know for sure, but the unusual (for Paul) absence of personal details in the letter supports a circular letter.

GOD LOVES WITH GRACE

The first foot in God's love for humans is the gift called grace, but grace has been misunderstood because it has been removed from its world and located into another world. John Barclay has corrected the situation for better understanding what Paul means by grace. I begin with his six dimensions of grace, each of which, or some of which, come into play when Paul uses terms connected to the idea of grace.

- First, God's grace is *superabundant* and magnificent and overflowing.
- Second, God's acts in grace toward us are *prior* to anything we say or do.
- Third, God *always* acts in grace.
- Fourth, God's grace is *effective* in what it is designed to do.
- Fifth, God's grace is distributed *without consideration of our worth or merit.*

- Sixth, God's grace can be *non-reciprocal*, which means God can show grace even when we refuse to respond. Of course, grace is also inherently *reciprocal*, that is, God gives, and we become agents of giving ourselves (Barclay, "Gift Perspective," 221–223).

Barclay makes it clear that not only do we need to give our attention to the dimensions of grace, but we also need to become alert to the pervasive idea of gift or grace in everything Paul writes. The fifth dimension, which expresses the *incongruity* of God's grace and our worth or merit, forms the heart of Paul's understanding of grace. Through and through, God's lavish grace to sinners is the platform on which Paul forms his message. It is why John Newton wrote his universally loved hymn, "Amazing Grace," and his story—from a reckless, impulsive youth, to a hideous level of participation in slavery as a slave trader, to one who comprehended his sin, to a much-loved pastor, and to a passionate fighter against slavery—illustrates very well the priority, superabundance, incongruity, and reciprocity of God's grace (see Hindmarsh, Borlase, *Amazing Grace*).

God's gracious love provides for us the forgiveness of sins (Ephesians 1:7). Notice, especially, that it is "in love" that we are adopted in Christ, and this all (and more) results in "the praise of his glorious grace" (1:4–6). Love is the energy in God that first prompts God's grace. But here is where we must begin: God first loves God's Son, the Lord Jesus Christ, and God's gracious love for us comes to us in Christ (1:6). I like how the *First Nations Version* translates "Christ": with "The Chosen One." The Hebrew and Greek terms behind "Christ" speak of someone being chosen and anointed for a special task. Esau McCaulley intensifies that idea: In Christ is a "physical and existential reality" because the existential is about faith and the physical about baptism and community fellowship. To be "in Christ" describes our union with Christ, our participation in the life of Christ, our relationship to Christ, as well as our embodied life and our relationship to all others in Christ. So, we turn to the dimensions of grace we experience in Christ.

Grace Words in Ephesians

Grace and peace to you from God our Father and the Lord Jesus Christ (1:2).

. . . to the praise of his glorious grace, which he has freely given us in the One he loves. In him we have redemption through his blood, the forgiveness of sins, in accordance with the riches of God's grace (1:6–7).

. . . made us alive with Christ even when we were dead in transgressions—it is by grace you have been saved (2:5).

. . . in order that in the coming ages he might show the incomparable riches of his grace, expressed in his kindness to us in Christ Jesus. For it is by grace you have been saved, through faith—and this is not from yourselves, it is the gift of God . . . (2:7–8).

Surely you have heard about the administration of God's grace that was given to me for you (3:2).

I became a servant of this gospel by the gift of God's grace given me through the working of his power.

> Although I am less than the least of all the Lord's people, this grace was given me: to preach to the Gentiles the boundless riches of Christ (3:7–8).
>
> But to each one of us grace has been given as Christ apportioned it (4:7).
>
> Do not let any unwholesome talk come out of your mouths, but only what is helpful for building others up according to their needs, that it may benefit those who listen (4:29).
>
> Be kind and compassionate to one another, forgiving each other, just as in Christ God forgave you (4:32).
>
> Grace to all who love our Lord Jesus Christ with an undying love (6:24).

GOD BLESSES IN CHRIST

We begin by blessing God along with Paul because God "has blessed us in the heavenly realms with every spiritual blessing in Christ" (1:3). The NIV opens verse three with "Praise," which is the adjective but same basic word as is found in both "blessed" and "blessing." Which is why I prefer the translation "Blessed is the God and Father . . . who blessed us with every Spirit-prompted blessing" (McKnight, *Second Testament*). God's blessing of us in Christ through the Spirit prompts us to bless God right back. The Greek word here is *eu* (good) + *logos* (word), which suggests speaking good words about God because he has done good things for us—in Christ! Even more, God's blessing does something in us, to us, and for us.

God's blessing occurs "in the heavenly realms," which is one of the favored expressions in Ephesians (1:3, 20–21; 2:6; 3:10; 6:12; cf. 4:9–10). This is Paul's parallel world/universe, where God and angels, both good and bad, dwell. What occurs there occurs here, so the heavenly realm does not suggest something we get in eternity but something occurring there as it is occurring here. The "every spiritual blessing" indicates the expansiveness and the superabundance of God's loving grace. God gives us all we want and more than we even know we want. In Christ, God welcomes us into the divine family, grants forgiveness, empowers us to participate meaningfully in God's family, and brings us into a unity with all God is doing in all creation.

GOD REDEEMS IN CHRIST

God's love for us prompts God to act for us in grace. The blessings of verse three are named in the verses that follow: God chooses us to be "holy and blameless" in God's own view of us; God predestines us to become, like Israel, God's family members ("family-placement" in *Second Testament*);* God gives us grace "freely" outside of our own worth and merit (don't we know it!); and God redeems us, or liberates us from

---

* The NIV at Ephesians 1:5 has "adoption to sonship," which in a note is clarified as the legal term for an "adopted male heir in Roman culture." Claire Powell, however, calls out a problem with the translation: "the rights and privileges normally accorded to adopted sons in those days are likened to the closeness of relationship God is willing to bestow on all who follow him. Therefore it is much clearer to use *children* in modern culture. The privileged relationship of the beloved child to a committed parent is in mind" (Powell, "Ephesians," 697). The Greek term is *huiothesia*, a combination of "son" and "placing/placement." A simple translation is "adoption," which the NIV has and which would have been adequate. The addition of "adoption *to sonship*" connects the term both to the Roman practice of adoption, to Israel as God's "son," and to inheritance rights for sons. Yet, Paul is not privileging men. See E. Heim, "Adoption," *Dictionary of Paul and His Letters*, ed. S. McKnight, L. Cohick, N.J. Gupta; 2nd edition (Downers Grove: IVP, 2023), 11–15.

the sin-prison, by the blood of Christ, which forgives us of our sins. Salvation words bleed from Paul's pen onto the parchment, and he has a hard time not blotting! And these are but a sampling of the richness of Paul's salvation terms. The idea of election, which is very much in harmony with God's election of Israel (covenant and release from captivity, or Genesis 12 and Exodus 11–12), but even more predestination, which is not so common, can be troubling. Some emphasize God's selection of some to be saved, and therefore of others not to be saved, while others—correctly—emphasize that election occurs in Christ, the Elect One. Mark Roberts wisely writes that these themes "do not serve as an invitation to debate but to worship" (Roberts, *Ephesians*, 26). He adds that the expression "in accordance with his pleasure and will" leads to this thought: "To put it simply, God chose us because that's what he decided to do, and doing so gave him pleasure. The more we consider God's delight in us, the more we will be drawn to worship" (26).

Redemption is from something into something else. We can reverse the "into" words to reveal the "from" ideas. We are chosen *into* "holy and blameless" *from* common, profane, and blameworthy conditions. We move *into* being predestined *from* (or *out of*) being those who otherwise would never experience God's grace. We move *into* God's family *from* being outside God's family. McCaulley observes that Paul's concerns are not "with what the Ephesians brought to the family" but what God makes of them in God's family (McCaulley, "Ephesians," 416). We move *into* God's freely-given grace in spite of our unworthiness *from* being those worthy only of God's non-grace, God's judgment. We move *into* a state of forgiveness *from* a state of remaining in our sin and death.

Barclay's term "incongruity" gets it exactly right. In Paul's cultural context status and honor mattered. In Paul's theology of grace neither status nor honor mattered. Correct that, both status and honor were flipped upside down so that those without status or honor before God, regardless of their status and honor in society, are given the highest of statuses and honors: "in the heavenly realms" (1:3).

All of this is in Christ. All because God loves us. All because God's love moves to us in grace. This grace is what forms unity among all believers.

God Unifies in Christ

God's design is to summon all humans and all creation and all the universe—heaven and earth—together. We call this unity, but Paul's term was bigger than that. We can translate his term with "recapitulating" or "to be absolutely complete" or "summing up all the plans God has for all creation." Paul's idea of God's loving and gracious salvation in Christ reveals God's "wisdom and understanding," that is, God's secret plan *in Christ* ("mystery of his will according to his good pleasure, which he purposed in Christ") to bring both Jews and gentiles into one body (1:9; 2:11–22; 3:6). As Claire Powell writes, "Christianity is not a religion in which the highest mysteries or blessings are reserved for a few. All believers, young and old, male and female, Jew and Gentile, are blessed with every spiritual blessing that heaven affords, and this has been in the mind of God from all eternity" (Powell, "Ephesians," 697).

From the moment of creation God's plan was to summon all things back together into a consummate unity. Sin divides; redemption unifies. Racism is sin; celebrating race in mutual affirmation is grace. Divisions emerge from people thinking they are superior; unity is formed when we realize we are equal. The Christian's responsibility in the here and now is to live for and strive for that unity. Final redemption will be the unification of all things. When we reduce God's redemption to our personal salvation and promise of going to heaven, we substitute ourselves for Christ as the center of all creation. God's loving grace redeems all things. Individualism works against unity; God-centeredness forms unity. Someday all creation will be under the umbrella of God's loving grace.

Final Note

Ephesians 1:3–14 is one sentence of more than two hundred words. I have broken it up into two readings to keep our first reflection shorter. Anyway, 1:3–10 is already more expansive and superabundant than we can take in, so we will have to finish the fuller passage in our next reading.

Questions for Reflection and Application

1. What does it mean to "eulogize" God?

2. Which of the six attributes of grace quoted from Barclay is most surprising to you? Why?

3. How does our ability to be unified with other believers effect our ability to be "in Christ"?

4. In what ways do individualism, division, sin, and superiority keep you from being unified with others in Christ?

5. How can a reminder of our calling from God help us withstand verbal attacks?

FOR FURTHER READING

John Barclay, "The Gift Perspective on Paul," in
    S. McKnight, B.J. Oropeza, editors, *Perspectives on
    Paul: Five Views* (Grand Rapids: Baker Academic,
    2020), 219–236.
Bruce Hindmarsh, Craig Borlase, *Amazing Grace: The
    Life of John Newton and the Amazing Story Behind
    His Song* (Nashville: W/Thomas Nelson, 2023),
    a brief introduction to the book can be found at:
    https://scotmcknight.substack.com/p/biographies
    -are-not-all-the-same.

THE BEAUTY OF THE
GOD OF GRACE

Ephesians 1:11–14

*[11] In him **we** were also <u>chosen</u>, having been <u>predestined</u> according to the plan of him who works out everything in conformity with the purpose of his will, [12] in order that we, who were the first to put our hope in Christ, might be for the praise of his <u>glory</u>. [13] And **you** also were included in Christ when you heard the message of truth, the gospel of your salvation. When you believed, you were marked in him with a <u>seal</u>, <u>the promised Holy Spirit</u>, [14] who is a <u>deposit</u> guaranteeing our inheritance until the <u>redemption</u> of those who are God's <u>possession</u>—to the praise of his <u>glory</u>.*

Paul's theology, like coffee, is an acquired taste. In passages like the previous one and today's, Paul's theology is a straight, hot, dark bean, double shot of espresso. You either take it all in one gulp or you sip it for a half hour or more. Paul knots intense vocabulary with loops and bows into one long sentence (vv. 3–14), all the while pouring (into our espresso demitasse) his favorite ideas about God, Christ, salvation, and the church. As in the previous passage, God's acts are in italics with supporting words underlined about God's acts. We add a double underline for a special shift from "we" to "you," which we will explain in a moment. Which reminds us not to let ourselves get tied into knots of debate about predestination and the unacceptable idea that God chose some to be damned forever and ever, which some have argued in the history of the church. I like the beautiful reminder we get in the *First Nations Version* at verse eleven: "Creator is working out all the details."

Election in the Bible, if we begin in Genesis, is, first, a much bigger term than how it has been used at times in theological knot-tying debates and, second, much less concerned with individual salvation than we have sometimes heard. God elected Israel out of all the nations to be God's mission agents in the world. Christopher Wright, an Old Testament specialist, summarizes God's election of Israel in these terms: "*The election of Israel is instrumental, not an end in itself.* God did not choose Israel that they alone should be saved, as if the purpose of election terminated with them. They were chosen rather as the means by which salvation could be extended to others throughout the earth." Thus, election is election *to mission* (Wright, *Mission of God*, 263). When the Bible mentions election and predestination, then, we may need to remind ourselves about the beautiful *purpose* of election.

THE PURPOSE OF ELECTING PREDESTINATION

To grasp the purpose, we need to read two verses at once (1:11–12). In this passage, God's loving grace that prompts inheritance and predestination has a goal: "in order that we . . . might be for the praise of his glory." It would be rash to wipe out all senses of salvation in these terms, but it is even more rash to narrow election to "you get saved, that person does not." The election is to an inheritance to be part of the people of God, in the plan of God, for the future of God. The intent of the "inheritance" (1:11, *Second Testament*, ESV; the NIV has "chosen") here is to form a people that give glory and honor back to God. They glorify God because of God's love-based grace to all creation. God, who is altogether beautiful, asks that recipients of grace acknowledge the Source of grace. Remember, too, that election occurs in Christ because Christ is the Elect One (Luke 9:35; Ephesians 1:4).

Every time you turn to God in thanks, lift your heart and hands to God in adoration, open your mouth to confess God's love for us, or sing the songs of glory to God, you *express your election*. The elect praise God; in praising God we are the elect.

THE MANNER OF ENTERING INTO ELECTION

Our strong espresso continues. The emphasis of Ephesians 1:3–14 undoubtedly falls in the direction of God's love and grace toward us in redeeming us. Emphases can become over-emphases. Paul makes it abundantly clear that we all have a response-ability in this grand and glorious redemption that God works in us. The "we" who are redeemed are "the ones who have first hoped" in Christ (1:12; *Second Testament*). The meaning of "we" and "first" are disputed, but one good possibility is that he's referring to Jewish believers, as in Romans 1:16. But Paul is not drawing a line down the middle aisle, with one sign designated for Jewish and the other for gentile believers. No, Paul wants them to see the beauty of "what they share in common Christ" (Roberts, *Ephesians*, 32). And, hoping is tied to the gentiles "when you believed" the "message of truth" that they had heard preached (Ephesians 1:13). Hoping in Christ is more than the hope sports fans have of a bottom place team getting to the top, when they know fully well the chances are thinner than slim. Hoping for Paul means setting one's hope fully on the redemption that is in Christ and trusting the God who has promised to redeem all creation (1:18; 2:12; 4:4). Thus, believing can be seen as hope, or hope the inevitable forward-looking side of faith. Both are true.

God reciprocates our act of faith, trust, and words of allegiance to Jesus with the gift of the Holy Spirit, the transforming Agent of God in this world. This Spirit marks them with a "seal," like circumcision (Romans 4:11), for that hoping faith's future complete and final consummation of salvation. When God is all in all, and Christ rules. That inner sense of God's Spirit at work in us is the "guaranteeing [of] our inheritance" (Ephesians 1:14). The Spirit is a down payment, or deposit, in our account that the rest of the payment is sure to arrive. Leonard Allen, in his beautiful memoir, connects the Father to love, Jesus to God's art form, and the Spirit as "beautifier." He writes, "Through the experience of created beauty, the Spirit awakens in us the desire for the wholeness, the *shalom*, of the age to come. . . . The beauty we discern now is a preview, given by the Spirit, of a beauty yet to come in the new heaven and the new earth." When we glimpse moments of this beauty, Allen asks, "Who could not be moved? And not only moved. Caught up. Caught up in the God of beauty. Caught up in the Great Story, the story we believe to be the true story of the world" (Allen, *The Bookroom*, 156, 157).

Once we acquire a taste for Paul's theology, we realize that salvation now is only part of the fullness of salvation. The fullness arrives after the Second Coming when the kingdom of God is established, when New Jerusalem descends to earth, when the New Heavens and the New Earth are formed. Election is knotted into the beauty of that Story.

QUESTIONS FOR REFLECTION
AND APPLICATION

1. What does it mean that God "elected" Israel to participate in mission?

2. How does worship relate to election here?

3. How do election and inheritance interact in this section?

4. What role does the Holy Spirit play in election?

5. In what ways has this section challenged or confirmed your previous understanding of election?

FOR FURTHER READING

Leonard Allen, *The Bookroom: Remembrance and Forgiveness—A Memoir* (Abilene: Abilene Christian University Press, 2024).

Christopher J.H. Wright, *The Mission of God: Unlocking the Bible's Grand Narrative* (Downers Grove: IVP Academic, 2006).

PRAYER TO THE GOD OF GRACE

Ephesians 1:15–23

[15] For this reason, ever since I heard about your faith in the Lord Jesus and your love for all God's people, [16] I have not stopped giving thanks for you, remembering you in my prayers. [17] I keep asking that the God of our Lord Jesus Christ, the glorious Father, may give you the Spirit of wisdom and revelation, so that you may know him better. [18] I pray that the eyes of your heart may be enlightened in order that you may know the hope to which he has called you, the riches of his glorious inheritance in his holy people, [19a] and his incomparably great power for us who believe. [19b] That power is the same as the mighty strength [20] he exerted when he raised Christ from the dead and seated him at his right hand in the heavenly realms, [21] far above all rule and authority, power and dominion, and every name that is invoked, not only in the present age but also in the one to come. [22] And God placed all things under his feet and appointed him to be head over everything for the church, [23] which is his body, the fullness of him who fills everything in every way.

Some people become known by their prayers. In talking about her grandfather, Willa Cather's narrator, Jim Burden, said this about his grandfather's prayers on Christmas morning: "Grandfather's prayers were often very interesting. He had the gift of simple and moving expression. Because he talked so little, his words had a peculiar force; they were not worn dull from constant use. His prayers reflected what he was thinking about at the time, and it was chiefly through them that we got to know his feelings and his views about things." Her grandfather loved the Lord and the Bible. On that Christmas morning, "He read the chapters from Saint Matthew about the birth of Christ, and as we listened, it all seemed like something that had happened lately, and near at hand. . . . He gave thanks for our food and comfort, and he prayed for the poor and destitute and great cities, where the struggle for life was harder than it was here with us" (Cather, *My Ántonia*, 67).

Prayers can be revealing. For me it is a pity I hear so many critical comments about the apostle Paul, as if he were some nasty missionary administrator commandeering everyone here and there. A man with a hard heart can't pray like the apostle Paul. Prayers reveal hearts. Paul's heart is supple and strong, hopeful and well-used.

So, today, I want to dip into four features of Paul's thanksgiving, four features that can instruct us in our praying habits. Before we turn there, the operative words in this prayer—and Paul wound the preliminaries up for one whole verse before he got to the words—are "I have not stopped giving thanks" or "I don't stop thanking" (1:16; NIV and *Second Testament*). The Greek word we translate with "thanks" is *eucharisteō*, a word built on two words—the first good (*eu*) and the second grace (*charis*). I like to translate it as "gracing" for a fresh angle. Paul describes a God who seemingly releases a ball in a pinball machine of thanks. God pings grace to Paul, Paul to the Ephesians, the Ephesians to Paul, and Paul back to God in good-gracing (thanking) God for the pinging joys of grace. Now to four ideas about prayer.

PERSONAL

In prayer, Paul goes personable. In verses fifteen to nineteen I circled in my NIV fifteen personal pronouns (I, my, you, your, and one "us"). Paul makes prayer for the Ephesians a personal connection. He prays out of his knowing of them: "ever since I heard about your faith in the Lord Jesus and your love for all God's people" (1:15). The *First Nations Version* amplifies "Lord Jesus" into "Creator Sets Free (Jesus)." They've tapped on an important but neglected key in the meaning of Lord: this Lord truly sets people free. Paul knows that their faith journeys are into this freedom. He's not like the priest reading a set liturgical prayer in front of him in which he has scratched in a caret (^), above which he pens in the name of the person he's been told to pray for. Paul knows these folks so well his prayers are tailored to them and to them alone. They were known for loving one another, though Revelation will reveal to us this very church lost its love (Revelation 2:4).

Before Kris and I eat our evening meal we not only give thanks to God for our food, but we pray for our family and for others who have expressed needs to us or who have asked us to pray for them: John, Mike, Nancy, Mary, Taylor, Becky. Names make prayer personal and the pray-er personable as naming names transcends the pious-sounding "bless our families and friends." When we at times tell someone we have been praying for them, they often express a warm affection of thanks. The Ephesians, or whoever heard this letter read, will have pushed the button in the pinball machine to ping the grace of thanksgiving back to Paul.

MEDIATED

Prayer mediates. Paul takes the Ephesians before God in thanking God for them, but he informs the Ephesians he's saying good things about them to God. Even if Paul's "I have not stopped thanking" has no object, the object in all of Paul's thanks-givings is God (cf. Romans 1:8; 1 Corinthians 1:4; Philippians 1:3; Colossians 1:3; 1 Thessalonians 1:2; 2 Thessalonians 1:3; 1 Timothy 1:12; 2 Timothy 1:3; Philemon 4). Thanking is not all Paul is doing for the Ephesians before God.

Paul's thanksgivings morph into mediated petitions. He thanks, he then remembers, and then he asks (Ephesians 1:16–17). One of the great Protestant doctrines is the priest-hood of all believers, that is, the direct, unmediated, and full access to God for every believer in Christ. Yet even here our priestly access to God is, like all graces, only available "in Christ." The freshness of this idea does not counter Israel's non-accessibility to God or of God's inaccessibility to only priests. Rather, the priesthood of Christ and our being in Christ makes us all priests (as Peter teaches at 1 Peter 2:5, 9). Which means we are given the ministry of mediating between God and humans, and humans and God—and praying is the primary act of mediation. We are so used to this privilege we can become numb to the glories of it: we are privileged in Christ to take others into the presence of God. *Here's Mike, O God, take care of his family. Here's Becky, Father, strengthen her for today, gracing her wounds.*

Abstract

Paul's prayer requests can sound abstract in what he asks for. Mark Roberts, after many years as a pastor, admits "Most of us don't pray like this" because "We tend to pray for immedi-ate needs" (Roberts, *Ephesians*, 51). He petitions the "glorious Father" to give to them "the Spirit of wisdom and revelation" (1:17). The answer to that rather abstract prayer request leads to the Ephesians knowing God better. Knowing God better correlates with knowing that God is revealed in Jesus Christ, looking for God in Bible reading, listening to God in prayer, learning about God as God works among God's people, and exulting in the glory of God in the grandeur of creation. If it were all reduced to reading the Bible, Paul would have said that. Instead, he began with "the Spirit of wisdom and revelation." Paul expects the Spirit to reveal to us the wisdom of God. Again, Mark Roberts: "knowing God, therefore, isn't something fixed and static, some list of facts that we master and then move on to other things. Rather, it is a lifelong growing in our understanding and experience of God" and "there is always more to be known" (Roberts, *Ephesians*, 55–56).

Knowing God is fleshed out in these words: "that the eyes of your heart may be enlightened in order that you may know the hope to which he has called you, the riches of his glorious inheritance in his holy people, and his incomparably great power for us who believe" (1:18–19). I want to reduce these abstractions to their basic senses. First, Paul prays for them to know God, which can only happen through the Holy Spirit who provides wisdom and revelation. Second, Paul prays they will become absorbed in the Christian Story's Christian hope, which means living now in the confidence that God will grant them the grand inheritance in the kingdom. Remember, the inheritance Paul has in mind is to be part of the people of God, in the plan of God, for the future of God. Third, Paul prays they will experience the power of God in their life. Thus, Paul prays for: Know God. Live in the Christian hope. Experience God's power. I now finish what Mark Roberts wrote above: "Our problem isn't that we pray for too many tiny needs; it's that we don't pray for enough big ones" (Roberts, *Ephesians*, 51). Amen.

People who pray for others would be wise to compare their prayer requests to Paul's, but not to learn they might fall short. No, pondering our prayers alongside Paul's reveals how connected ours actually are to wanting others to know God, wanting others to live out the Christian hope, and wanting others to experience God's power. Paul's terms, I have said, are abstract. Perhaps it would be better to say his terms are wide and deep terms for what humans most want out of this life.

SIDETRACKED

Paul's theology and style, as we wrote in the previous passage, are an acquired taste. In the middle of verse nineteen Paul is unleashed, and he wanders from his prayer request to an extrapolation of what he means by the power of God. It's a sidebar of a sidetracked apostle, who has fallen in love with the God whose power he has experienced over and over. In a word, the abundant "power" (*dunamis*) available to believers (1:19a) is the "energy" (*energeia*) of God that God "energized" (*energeō*) in the resurrection and ascension of Jesus Christ (1:19b–20; *Second Testament*). What a claim! Believers have access to resurrection and ascension energies and powers.

The Importance of the Ascension

"Thus in Jesus' ascension God has (1) reconciled the world to himself, (2) restored the immortal human glory of his image-bearing children, (3) empowered those eschatologically 'seated in the heavenly realms in Christ Jesus' (Eph 2:6 NIV) with the life of his Spirit, and (4) guaranteed the consummation of heaven and earth in union with God."

Cherith Fee Nordling, Becky Castle Miller, "Ascension," in *The Dictionary of Paul and His Letters*, 2d ed. (Downers Grove: IVP Academic, 2023), 53–57, quoting from p. 57.

Theologian that he is, Paul sidetracks his concentration from believers' having access to these powers to the exalted status of Jesus Christ at the right hand of God (1:20–22; cf. Mark 10:35–45). His description is effusive: "above all celestial leadership and authority and power and lordship and [above] every name being named not only in this Era but in the coming Era." This language labels Jesus as the Emperor over all empire-less emperors, the King over all kingdom-less kings, and the Lord over all lordless lords. When God's energy raised and exalted Jesus to these supernal heights, God, not in some far-off future, but simultaneously "placed all things under his feet" (Ephesians 1:22). Right now, whether this world looks like it or not, Paul claims, Jesus rules over all. As the Lord of lords, the Father gave the Son the gift to be "head over everything for the church" (1:22–23). This, too, is a remarkable claim: God gave Christ (1) to be the head over everything, and (2) this gift of Christ was to or for the church. As such, Christ is the head of the whole church, not just one group or one race or one gender in the church that happens to think it is the one true and faithful embodiment of the church, which far too many have claimed.

Paul has run out of subordinates, so he sums it all up with "the fullness of the one filling all things in all ways" (1:23; *Second Testament*). These words are about the pervasive presence of Christ in the world through his presence in the church (see 1:10). The center of all creation for the Lord of Lords and King of Kings is the church, but the church is the body of Christ, which means the fullness turns all our attention to Christ (cf. Colossians 1:15–20).

QUESTIONS FOR REFLECTION
AND APPLICATION

1. What do you observe about Paul's heart as you read his prayers?

2. How does Paul serve as a mediator between God and other people?

3. List some of the things Paul prays for the people he loves. How do those compare or contrast with your prayers?

4. Take a moment to pray a personal prayer for someone who has asked you to pray for them, or for someone you know needs prayer. Express the grace of thanksgiving and love in your prayer.

5. Think about a time you have heard someone pray in a way that revealed their beautiful heart. What did you notice about their prayer?

FOR FURTHER READING

Willa Cather, *My Ántonia*, intro. Lucy Hughes-Hallett, Everyman's Library 228 (New York: Alfred A. Knopf, 1996).

LOVE BECOMES A BUNDLE OF GRACES

Ephesians 2:1–10

¹ As for you, you were dead in your transgressions and sins, ² in which you used to live when you followed the ways of this world and of the ruler of the kingdom of the air, the spirit who is now at work in those who are disobedient. ³ All of us also lived among them at one time, gratifying the cravings of our flesh and following its desires and thoughts. Like the rest, we were by nature deserving of wrath.

*⁴ But because of <u>his great love for us, God, who is rich in mercy</u>, ⁵ **made us alive with Christ even when we were dead in transgressions**—<u>it is by grace you have been saved</u>. ⁶ And **God raised us up** with Christ and **seated us with him in the heavenly realms in Christ Jesus**, ⁷ in order that in the coming ages he might show the incomparable riches of his grace, expressed in **his kindness to us in Christ Jesus**.*

⁸ <u>For it is by grace you have been saved</u>, through faith—and this is not from yourselves, it is the gift of God—⁹ not by works, so that no one can boast.

¹⁰ For we are God's handiwork, created in Christ Jesus to do good works, which God prepared in advance for us to do.

Some homes in our village look fatigued and bored. The local lingo is these are "tear-down homes." On our walks we pass by some of these homes daily. The pattern has become common. One day we find the entire lot of a wearied home fenced off. Soon the wreckers arrive to break it apart, level it to the ground, with the wreckage towed away. (At times they save a corner of the former basement's walls so they can slide by ordinances about "impervious coverage.") Surveying and grading and digging and cement pouring are followed by a gradual construction of what soon looks like a gorgeous home. The old and the new. No matter how comfortable that old home was at one time, it was unsalvageable, so a new one was in order. At times, Kris and I will mutter to one another that the new owners had a vision for what that spot could become and so saved the lot, turning it into a work of beauty.

Transfer that demolition and transformation scene into human beings, and you have today's reading about the saving work of God's grace. If you read today's passage slowly it moves from "dead in your transgressions and sins" to our becoming "God's handiwork" (2:1, 10). I love that Paul mixes up "you" with "we." He moves from "you were dead" to "All of us" to "like the rest of us" and to God's love "for us" and "you have been saved." He does this because he knows he is as much, if not more, of a recipient of God's loving grace as they are. In the middle is God's love, so we begin there.

BUT BECAUSE OF HIS GREAT LOVE . . .

In spite of the worn-out condition of humans, whom Paul says are dead in the water of their sins, God loves us (2:4). God worked in us "even when we were dead in transgressions"

(2:5). Love is at times mistakenly connected only to grace, as if God hated us but then Christ stepped in so God could love us again. No, God loves us "even when" we are in our sins. And it is "because" of God's love for us in our sinful condition that God's grace comes our way.

Elements of Grace

1. God's grace is *superabundant* and magnificent and overflowing.
2. God acts in grace toward us *prior* to anything we say or do.
3. God *always* acts in grace.
4. God's grace is *effective* in what it is designed to do.
5. God's grace is distributed *without consideration of our worth or merit.*
6. God's grace can be *non-reciprocal*, which means God can show grace even when we refuse to respond. Of course, grace is also inherently *reciprocal*, that is, God gives, and we become agents of giving ourselves.

(Barclay, "Gift Perspective," 221–223).

Grace, then, is not an abstract theological concept. Grace is what love looks like when God's love is turned toward humans trapped in their sinful ways. First comes love, then comes grace. To tap into the elements of grace sketched earlier (see the Elements of Grace), I have marked in today's reading how four of the elements about God's grace appears: *incongruous*, superabundant, ***prior***, and especially effective in what it is designed to do. (Notice that "prior" is both italicized and bold because it is both incongruous and prior.) To be sure, each of us might assign some of these terms and lines to a different category, but that only proves the point: grace is a bundle of graces all at once. One element of grace shines a bit brighter than another at this point, but at different moments some other element shines brighter. As an example of how effusive grace actually is, take a look at "through faith" in verse eight. Is this God's prior action in us through the Spirit (yes), or the incongruity of God's loving grace toward us even when we are sinners (yes), or is "through faith" the effectiveness of grace in us (yes)?

As for You . . .

We are all tear-down projects. The words Paul uses are as strong as they are clear. First, their condition: "dead in your transgressions and sins," which the *First Nations Version* expresses wonderfully with "We all once walked a dark and crooked path that led us to death." Second, they are responsible for how they lived: "in which you used to live when you followed the ways of this world and of the ruler of the kingdom of the air." Third, they are responsible for their disordered desires: "gratifying the cravings of our flesh and following its desires and thoughts." He takes us to our own depths when he says, "we were by nature anger's children" (*Second Testament*), though the NIV intensifies it too much when it adds "deserving" (2:3). These terms are echoed in the second half of today's reading when we come to "this isn't from you" and "so someone might not boast" (2:8, 9; *Second Testament*). F. Scott Spencer puts this all into a wonderful formula: "Paul is absorbed by God's *grace*, God's *gift*, in Christ. Grace (*charis*) sources his and others' gifts (*charismata*), leaving no room for boasting or boosterism" (Spencer, *Seven Challenges*, 21).

We are responsible for our own sins and desires, as well

as the condition that results from our choices (death and God's judgment). We have been co-opted by a cosmic agent of sin, and Paul surely has in mind Satan and its minions. Because of our condition we are unable to lift ourselves out of our own condition, and because we can do nothing to save ourselves, we have no legs to stand on to shout out our boastings. *We find ourselves in this very condition when we encounter the God who loves us and graciously acts to turn death into life.*

What ought to scare us to death is the idea of justice, where everyone gets what they deserve—no more and no less. But God's love first deals grace. As Marilynne Robinson once wrote in an essay about reconciliation in final scenes in Shakespeare, "What happens in these scenes is no sorting out of grievances, no putting of things right. Justice as that word is normally understood has no part in them. They are about forgiveness that is unmerited, unexpected, unasked, unconditional. In other words, they are about grace" (Robinson, *The Givenness of Things*, 39).

God . . . Made Us Alive

Paul raids his dictionary to describe not only our sins but also God's love-based grace. This God loves us and is "rich in mercy" (2:4), and out of that loving mercy God "made us alive *with* Christ" (in his resurrection; cf. 1:19–20). Giving us a life means God "saved us" from death, transgressions, sins, and God's anger over what we have done to ourselves (2:5–6). As that great Methodist scholar-preacher, C.K. Barrett, once said in a sermon, "the New Testament is not a book of morals or religion, but of God's wondrous love in saving lost humankind. 'Being saved' may have an old-fashioned ring to it these days, but it is one of the old-fashioned things the church has to relearn in every generation" (Barrett, *Luminescence* 2.190).

Barrett's old-fashioned idea reminds us that God saves us from the guilt and power of sin (*Luminescence* 2.193).

In raising us, God not only opened death's grave for a resurrection, but God exalted us—again with Christ—and "seated us with him in the heavenly realms" (2:6), or as the *First Nations Version* renders it, "the highest place in the spirit-world." This ought to awaken us: we *are right now sitting next to Jesus in the Throne Room of God*! This ought also to grab our attention: we live now both on earth and in the heavenlies, we live in the Now and in the Future.

God raised us up so that, in the Future, in Christ God could "exhibit . . . his grace's excessive wealth and graciousness for us" (2:7; *Second Testament*). We will all be trophy-children of God in the kingdom of God. All of us. That's our Future. In the Now, "we are his compositions," which I prefer to the NIV's less literary "handiwork" (2:10). The former is a literary image, the latter the work of an artisan or a builder. What makes up our compositions? "Good works" that God creates through us in Christ Jesus. As the *First Nations Version* paraphrases the expressions, "We are like clay in his hands, molded from the Chosen One [Jesus], made to be like him." In a previous passage, I mentioned John Newton, the former slave trader whose conversion led him—as it should him and all of us—to begin perceiving both the superabundance of God's grace but also his "composition" life that created in Christ the hymn "Amazing Grace" (Hindmarsh, Borlase, *Amazing Grace*).

Knowing God's love, all of our "as for you's," and that God is in the work of giving us a new life, Stanley Hauerwas once wrote up this prayer:

> Are we yet alive, Lord? We feel pain, sorrow, happiness.
> We cry, wail, laugh. Are these signs that we are alive?
> Or are they but death—gurgles masquerading as signs

of life? We find it hard to believe, to understand, that we come to life through being baptized into your son's good death. Yet you have made us your baptized, giving us life, life that makes our pain, sorrow and happiness real. Life that makes our crying, wailing and laughing service to one another. Raise us, then, from our watery graves shouting, "Jesus Christ is Lord!" so that the world may see your liveliness, your love. AMEN. (Hauerwas, *Prayers Plainly Spoken*, 22)

A tragedy in the church is the reduction of grace to "you are going to hell . . . but you're also lucky that God still loves you, so repent from your awfulness and trust the cross of Christ." Grace in Paul sure does emphasize our sinful condition, but God's grace comes to us because *God loves us* and because God *wants to demolish* our tear-down condition and God *wants to create an entirely new composition* out of us. And, as Barrett preached, "grace is not a theological definition, but God's action in Jesus Christ, and what grace means you can learn best from Jesus" (Barrett, *Luminescence* 2.191). Grace, then, is an effective power to make us into God-honoring images that display the love of God in this world. Anything less is a tragedy.

QUESTIONS FOR REFLECTION AND APPLICATION

1. What surprises you most about grace in this section?

2. What is the connection between love and grace here?

3. If you were to consider yourself God's "composition," what story do you see God writing in and with your life?

4. How does it feel to consider we are "responsible for our own sins and desires" and "unable to lift ourselves out of our own condition"?

5. Describe how it then feels to recognize the power and efficacy of God's grace to lift us and free us.

FOR FURTHER READING

John Barclay, "The Gift Perspective on Paul," in S. McKnight, B.J. Oropeza, editors, *Perspectives on Paul: Five Views* (Grand Rapids: Baker Academic, 2020), 219–236.

C.K. Barrett, Fred Barrett, *The Sermons of C.K. and Fred Barrett: Luminescence*, volume 2, ed. Ben Witherington III (Eugene: Cascade, 2017), 190–193.

Stanley Hauerwas, *Prayers Plainly Spoken* (Downers Grove: IVP, 1999).

Bruce Hindmarsh, Craig Borlase, *Amazing Grace: The Life of John Newton and the Amazing Story Behind His Song* (Nashville: W/Thomas Nelson, 2023), a brief introduction to the book can be found at: https://scotmcknight.substack.com/p/biographies -are-not-all-the-same.

Marilynne Robinson, *The Givenness of Things: Essays* (New York: Farrar, Straus and Giroux, 2015).

F. Scott Spencer, *Seven Challenges That Shaped the New Testament: Understanding the Inherent Tensions of Early Christian Faith* (Grand Rapids: Baker Academic, 2024).

GRACE TRANSCENDS ETHNICITIES

Ephesians 2:11–22

[11] Therefore, remember that formerly you who are Gentiles by birth and called "uncircumcised" by those who call themselves "the circumcision" (which is done in the body by human hands)—[12] remember that at that time you were separate from Christ, excluded from citizenship in Israel and foreigners to the covenants of the promise, without hope and without God in the world. [13] But now in Christ Jesus you who once were far away have been brought near by the blood of Christ.

[14] For he himself is our peace, who has made the two groups one and has destroyed the barrier, the dividing wall of hostility, [15] by setting aside in his flesh the law with its commands and regulations. His purpose was to create in himself one new humanity out of the two, thus making peace, [16] and in one body to reconcile both of them to God through the cross, by which he put to death their hostility. [17] He came and preached peace to you who were far away and peace to those who were near. [18] For through him we both have access to the Father by one Spirit.

[19] Consequently, you are no longer foreigners and strangers, but fellow citizens with God's people and also members of his household, [20] built on the foundation of the apostles and prophets, with

Christ Jesus himself as the chief cornerstone. [21] In him the whole building is joined together and rises to become a holy temple in the Lord. [22] And in him you too are being built together to become a dwelling in which God lives by his Spirit.

Laura, our daughter, teaches at a grade school that in any given year can have more than three dozen different language groups and ethnicities. Ethnicities are culturally shaped groups of people based on heritage or ancestry, and ethnicities are both bigger than and narrower than the human-constructed, physically based ideas of race. In the first century, a Jewish author like Paul had been socialized to think of two major ethnicities in the world: Jews and gentiles. Paul was surely more alert than that in some of his travels, but his operative category for ethnicity, which shows up especially in Galatians and Romans, was the Jew-gentile division. We can begin right there for reading today's passage well. Paul believes God, in Christ, at least partly deconstructs divisions based on ethnicity.

It has been said that racism is America's original sin. If so, its original sin is the ethnicity ideology of white supremacy that degrades those with a skin color that is non-white or with a culture unlike theirs. America's history of pushing Native Americans off their land, enslaving Africans, and disinheriting Mexicans from their homes and land was accomplished by people who mostly claimed to be Christians. Some were crusaders and some were politicians, but all were exploiters *on the basis of ethnicity and race.* Robert Chao Romero writes about the negative sense many Chicana/o persons feel about the church, which "is grounded in centuries of historical and contemporary misrepresentation of the teachings of Jesus. In a very real sense, the history of Latinas/os in the Americas is one of systemic racism perpetuated by white individuals claiming to be Christian" (Romero, *Brown Church*, 6). As an African American friend of mine has often said, "We wear our uniform and can never take it off." The uniform of which he speaks is his skin color. Mitzi Smith writes, "African Americans are all too familiar with 'barriers of separation' that historically and currently attempt to limit our full participation as US citizens" (Smith, "Ephesians–2 ed," 375). No passage in the New Testament exposes the sins of racism and claims to ethnic superiority any more clearly than today's passage. Walking through the passage with Paul will both expose and enlighten us.

How Paul Understands Gentiles

Paul operates on the basis of a strong, if not harsh, ethnic bias about gentiles. The *First Nations Version* translates the term behind "gentiles" as "Nations" and in *The Second Testament* I use "ethnic groups." For Paul they are "gentiles" on the basis of their "flesh," though the NIV translates it "gentiles by birth." As such, Paul deems them with his fellow Jews as the "uncircumcised." Gentiles, *qua* gentiles, are "separate from Christ" if they do not have faith in Christ and, as gentiles, they are "rendered as 'others' from Yisraēl's communal-life and foreigners of the pledge's covenants." Even more, they have no "hope" and are "atheists" and thus "far away" (2:11–13). My translations from *The Second Testament* attempt to echo the jagged edges of Paul's language, while the *First Nations Version* helpfully frames these terms with "You Outside Nations." Paul's perception of gentiles then touches upon spiritual condition, ethnicity, and race. The Ephesian believers were almost certainly not offended by Paul's descriptors. Ethnic observations about others were common in the ancient world, and slurs and

41

labels were traded back and forth. That does not mean labels don't deserve to be brought into the light.

If you think Paul's world was into labeling others too much, read this paragraph from Robert Chao Romero—professor, lawyer, pastor—who has himself been labeled time and time again:

> I am an Asian-Latino or "Chino-Chicano," historian, lawyer, and evangélico pastor (in the Latin American tradition, and to be fiercely distinguished from American evangelicalism). I was born in East Los Angeles to a Mexican immigrant father and Chinese immigrant mother. I was raised in the small San Gabriel Valley town of Hacienda Heights. I was called "beaner" as a child and denied access to gifted learning programs in the recently desegregated public schools of Los Angeles. In sharing my ambition to become a lawyer, I was told in high school, "I'd never hire a Mexican lawyer." I was also told by my high school counselor that I should consider the local state school instead of UCLA. I went on to receive my PhD in Latin American history from UCLA and my JD from UC Berkeley, and I have been a professor of Chicana/o studies and Asian American studies at UCLA since 2005. I was ordained "in the hood" by black and Latino multidenominational Christian pastors of South Los Angeles, and, together with my wife, Erica, I've been a pastor to activist students for more than a decade as part of our Jesus 4 Revolutionaries ministry. Over the years I have experienced racial microaggressions by professors, church congregants, activists of the left and right, hateful internet trolls, realtors, and police. (Romero, *Brown Church*, 18)

The man is a Christian, a pastor, a professor, a lawyer—and because of his skin color and ethnicity he has experienced ethnic bias and racism, often at the hands of Christians. Ephesians 2 haunts the oppressors. There is no grace at work in how he has been labeled.

How Paul Understands Jews

Paul, both from patriotism and from his covenant thinking, thought of Jews as a special people. They are God's elect (cf. Genesis 12 and Ephesians 1:3–14). In our passage his sense of pride in Israel appears in "the circumcision" (2:11), though he concedes it is a circumcision done by hand and not of the heart or in the Spirit (cf. Romans 2:25–29; Colossians 2:11–12). Even more, election leads to gentile exclusion from the political and communal life of Israel, as well as to perceiving all gentiles as "foreigners to the covenants of promise," which means his fellow Jews are part of Israel, they inherit those covenants, and they have hope and connection to God. They are those who are "near" to God (Ephesians 2:12–17).

The emphasis of this passage does not stop with this division of humans into two radically separate ethnic groups: Jews and gentiles. In fact, Paul can be accused of hyperbole for the purpose of exalting the superabundance of God's loving grace that knocks down what divides Jews and gentiles.* Hyperbole or not, his worldview was shaped by these divisions for Paul.

---

* For those who have heard about the academic discussions about Paul, the bringing together of Jews and gentiles in Christ and in the church is the heartbeat of what is called the "new perspective." For discussions of this, see Scot McKnight, B.J. Oropeza, eds., *Perspectives on Paul: Five Views* (Grand Rapids: Baker Academic, 2020). The new perspective chapter was written by our (B.J. and my) professor, James D.G. Dunn, who has been called the father of the new perspective.

How Paul Understands
"in Christ"

Everything changed in Christ. Everything changes with God's love that comes to us in grace. Here is one of many summary statements by Paul of what happens in Christ: Gentiles who were "far away have been brought near," in grace, "by the blood of Christ" (2:13). Another way of saying it comes next: "for he himself is our peace, who has made the two groups one and has destroyed the barrier" (2:14). The barrier is the law as interpreted in that day, a law that distinguished Jews and gentiles on the basis of God's covenant relationship with Israel (2:14, 16). Esau McCaulley reminds us that the law "divided people. Christ's death nullified the law in the sense that it can no longer play that role." Even more, sin hijacked the law and turned it against God's purposes (McCaulley, "Ephesians," 419–420). Again, "his purpose was to create in himself one new humanity out of the two, thus making peace, and in one body to reconcile both of them to God through the cross" (2:15–16). Thus, Christ is the peace (2:14) and makes a "peace treaty" (*First Nations*) with humans and declares peace with those who were "far away" and with those "who were near" (2:17), giving us all access, or a "clear path" (*First Nations*) to God. This is all the power of God's grace.

The place of grace-based peace is not subtle for Paul. The place of peace is Christ and only "in Christ" is this kind of peace between gentiles and Jews known. In other words, the one body that transcends these ethnic divisions emerges only through redemption. Paul believes the place of peace is the church, the body of Christ, the embodiment of the grace-life "in Christ." In him all ethnic groups become sisters and brothers. It is imperative for believers to work out this unity in the church and to extend it into society on the basis of exhibiting its powers in the church.

Is This Unifying Gospel Divisive?

Within the North American church, there exist streams and communities that not only ignore racism and sexism, but suggest that those individuals who promote justice in these arenas are being needlessly divisive. But we who believe that racism and sexism are sins that are doing real damage to the church are not causing division. We are taking the fall [and the gospel] seriously. If Christ's resurrection is real, then those sins do not have the last word. The resurrection gives us hope that no sin is more powerful than God.

Esau McCaulley, "Ephesians," 423.

Thus, Paul has a radically new perspective on gentile and Jewish believers, but his emphasis here is on gentiles (2:11, 19). His words are "Consequently," which is the consequence of being in Christ, "you are no longer foreigners and strangers, but fellow citizens with God's people and also members of his household" (2:19). You have to love the *First Nations Version* translation: "We are all related to one another and initiated into Creator's lodge that is built together with wooden poles"! In Romans, Paul's image is gentiles being grafted into the root stock of Israel (Romans 11:17–24). The church does not replace Israel; the church expands Israel by incorporating gentile believers in the Jewish Messiah. This new household is the church, and Christ is the "chief cornerstone," and the "apostles and prophets" are the "foundation" (Ephesians 2:20). Paul shows much less interest in the apostles and prophets than he does in Christ. Only "in him" a unity forms into a "holy temple" in which the promised expectation of God dwelling among his people again is created—and that happens in the Spirit (2:21–22). "The church is not held together by the preaching of Christ, but by Christ in their midst" (McCaulley, "Ephesians," 420). Our consistency with the gospel is made visible by how unified we are with one another. To the degree we are divided, to that same degree we have blocked the work of Christ.

A summary statement: only in the grace of Christ are these ethnic divisions overcome, not in a way that destroys ethnicities but in a way that "in Christ" transcends them. "Jesus becomes the great equalizer and common denominator" (Smith, "Ephesians–2 ed.," 375). Romero, to take but one example, has shown the vision of a Christ-based activism for ethnic and racial justice has been part of the Latino/a community for five hundred years. Hear his words:

> In every instance of racial and social injustice in Latin America and the United States over the centuries, the Brown Church has challenged such great evils as the Spanish conquest and Spanish colonialism, the *sistema de castas* (caste system), Manifest Destiny and US settler colonialism in the Southwest, Latin American dictatorships, US imperialism in Central America, the oppression of farmworkers, and current exploitation and marginalization of undocumented immigrants.

He finishes that list of the Brown church's historic gospel-shaped activism in these words: "The Brown Church has done all of this in the name of Jesus" (Romero, *Brown Church*, 11).

Paul would say only under that umbrella can we genuinely overcome racism and ethnic supremacies. No one needs to hear this more than the American church today, which is predominantly a gentile church divided against itself. Sunday morning proves division every week. White supremacy, which has taken root in Christian nationalism, is on the rise (Whitehead, *American Idolatry*; Whitehead and Perry, *Taking America Back for God*). The next generation has become increasingly disaffected with the church over its complicity in white supremacy. We are not called to work to form this unity. Rather, we are called to live out the unity that already exists in Christ. The American church has rebuilt the walls Christ knocked down. Again, Esau McCaulley: "What Paul articulates here is a Christocentric, Spirit-filled community of faith whose life together is an enacted parable of the gospel" ("Ephesians," 421).

QUESTIONS FOR REFLECTION AND APPLICATION

1. How does Paul perceive gentiles?

2. How does Paul perceive Jews?

3. What does it mean for Jesus to function as the place of peace between peoples and ethnicities?

4. Consider how much racism and colonization has been perpetrated by people who call themselves Christians. How can you make sense of this?

5. How grace-shaped is your church when it comes to ethnic unity?

FOR FURTHER READING

Robert Chao Romero, *Brown Church: Five Centuries of Latina/o Social Justice, Theology, and Identity* (Downers Grove: IVP Academic, 2020).

Andrew Whitehead, *American Idolatry: How Christian Nationalism Betrays the Gospel and Threatens the Church* (Grand Rapids: Brazos, 2023).

Andrew Whitehead, Samuel Perry, *Taking America Back for God: Christian Nationalism in the United States* (New York: Oxford, 2020).

GRACE IS THE
MYSTERY

Ephesians 3:1–13

¹ For this reason I, Paul, the prisoner of Christ Jesus for the sake of you Gentiles—

² Surely you have heard about the administration of God's grace that was given to me for you, ³ that is, the mystery made known to me by revelation, as I have already written briefly. ⁴ In reading this, then, you will be able to understand my insight into the mystery of Christ, ⁵ which was not made known to people in other generations as it has now been revealed by the Spirit to God's holy apostles and prophets. ⁶ This mystery is that through the gospel the Gentiles are heirs together with Israel, members together of one body, and sharers together in the promise in Christ Jesus.

⁷ I became a servant of this gospel by the gift of God's grace given me through the working of his power. ⁸ Although I am less than the least of all the Lord's people, this grace was given me: to preach to the Gentiles the boundless riches of Christ, ⁹ and to make plain to everyone the administration of this mystery, which for ages past was kept hidden in God, who created all things. ¹⁰ His intent was that now, through the church, the manifold wisdom of God should be made known to the rulers and authorities in the heavenly realms, ¹¹ according to his eternal purpose that he accomplished in

Christ Jesus our Lord. [12] In him and through faith in him we may approach God with freedom and confidence. [13] I ask you, therefore, not to be discouraged because of my sufferings for you, which are your glory.

The problem we Christians face with the gospel of Paul is systemic. Our system. Our system is biased in favor of Whites. I'm part of the problem. I'm complicit. I can't see the problem. I need help to see it. The whiteness of our systems is invisible to Whites who are unconsciously, but intentionally and complicitly, privileged by the system. The gospel of Paul expanded the gospel to include anyone and everyone who believed in Jesus Christ. His gospel was given to him by God "for you," that is, for the gentiles. But entrance into his communities of faith was not the goal. Transformation of both the individual and the group, you and me and the church (local and universal), was the gospel's goal.

Paul's challenge is ours. He faced as much systemic ethnic bias as we do today. We need the gospel that was given to Paul for others. Our others may not be his, but the closer we look, the more we see his others are the same as our others. They are those who are not us.

Our systemic bias has become invisible. Those who deny it are in it. Those who work to make it visible will experience troubles. As Esau McCaulley has written, "Therefore, just as Paul was willing to risk going to prison, White pastors and churches must face the inevitable slander and misunderstanding that can arise when one partners with believers whose lives are impacted daily by injustice" (McCaulley, "Ephesians," 422).

We need a method that permits us to pull the truth about what stands behind the curtain of invisibility to make systemic bias visible. To get this onto the screen, I point to the evangelical Asian American Jeff Liou, child of Taiwanese immigrants, who points us to the mass shooting in Atlanta on March 16th, 2021. The church of the shooter did not take responsibility for how it shaped the shooter's "heart and mind." That church was complicit. The church folks did not see it. Their explanation was pure individualism with no regard for the systemic impact of a collective. An increasing number of Asians are experiencing racism in the US, and though the privileged want to claim the method for unveiling systemic ethnic bias and racism is "woke" or "liberal" or "progressive" in order to squash it, Liou and his co-author write about the method that we need, called Critical Race Theory (CRT), saying,

> To the contrary, CRT enables us to identify the ways in which certain theologies, in an ill-fated attempt to same-ify and flatten what God has made beautifully diverse, result in the most polite, psychological, and physical death dealing. . . . In order to condemn racism in all its forms, one must understand the novel, viral strains of racism that are emerging. CRT is actually indispensable in this regard because it, too, organizes and operational-izes the collective memories of racism and understanding of systems and structures that work against Asian Americans. (Romero, Liou, *Christianity*, 20)

Perhaps you think this introduction to today's reading is a tangent. It is not.

If the gospel is for all—and it is,
> If we are not multiethnic in both attendance and leadership—and we are not,
Then we need help.

We need Critical Race Theory for the sake of the gospel, the one the apostle Paul preached, to take root in the USA and in our churches. CRT presses us to ask who has power, what systems are in place, and how those systems pander to and prop up those who have the power—and oppress those who don't. The gospel shatters the protective powers of privilege. Ephesians reveals this shattering gospel.

Today's passage is Paul's own reflection about himself and his calling to be a gospel agent. Paul is a prisoner for this gospel, and he is suffering for this gospel (3:1, 13). He encourages the Ephesians not to be discouraged because the power of God is mightier than the prisons of the empire. Just ask Nelson Mandela or Martin Luther King, Jr., both of whose prison times became revolution times for the gospel of justice and freedom. In your asking and thinking about them, however, we need to keep in mind that no matter the good that may come from incarceration, today's incarceration in the USA is shaped by "racism, classism, and sexism" (Cohick, Proclamation, 53).

THE GOSPEL IS A MYSTERY

We need to keep our attention on the terms Paul uses for his gospel, and they come at us fast and furious. Plus, he repeats himself in the two paragraphs of today's reading (3:2–6, 7–13). God gave Paul, who did not deserve the vocation (3:8; cf. Acts 9:1–2; Galatians 1:13), a job description, an "administration" (NIV) or a responsibility at the level of "management" (*Second Testament*), and the task was to manage and administer grace "for you" or for the gentiles (3:2, 8). We need to pause to remind ourselves that our gifts from God that we are called to manage are not given to enhance our reputations or to build our brand. They are gifts given to us to pass on to others, not unlike the manager of a huge fund to supply the poor with tuition for college! Richard Bauckham, who has a great gift of writing, in his memoir about a vocation-threatening illness, wrote just prior to the arrival of that illness, "Keep me from self-importance, self-promotion, and possessiveness." He added as commentary to this prayer, "The greatest danger in a vocation is turning it from being for the glory of God to being a search for glory for oneself" (Bauckham, *Blurred Cross*, 42).

One of Paul's favorite terms for his gospel-for-the-gentiles, which incorporates them into Israel to fulfill the Abrahamic promise, is *mystery* (3:3, 6, 9), what one scholar calls "the plot twist that no one saw coming" (McCaulley, "Ephesians," 422). We are not to think of this as some special secret you and I as Christians share that we keep to ourselves. The mystery of this gospel has been "made known to [Paul] by revelation" (3:3), and he is now the agent of that mission in making it known from Jerusalem to Antioch to Ephesus to Corinth to Rome. It's an open secret that Paul both preaches the gospel to gentiles and brings them into unity with Jewish believers in Jesus (3:6). He has "insight" into how this works because God revealed it to him. But he's not alone: he knows this gospel has also been made known by the Spirit to the "apostles and prophets" (3:5).

The special feature of Paul's gospel mission was not known until God revealed it to him. Here are three historical facts: (1) the people of Israel, especially from the second century BCE onward, welcomed gentiles who wanted to observe the law of Moses, but (2) no one was like Paul in pursuing gentiles to embrace the Jewish Messiah, Jesus, and (3) his vision was that gentile believers were to become one with Jewish believers in Jesus. As such, then, Paul's mystery is not simply about evangelizing gentiles and then moving on. Paul's mystery enters into the mission of God in this world to evangelize, form churches, and disciple new believers and leads to a life of grace-based boundary-breaking unity (Fleming, "Mission," 703–704).

THE GOSPEL TAKES ROOT
IN LOCAL CHURCHES

The church is the room where it happens. Not the empire. God's "intent was that now, *through the church*, the manifold wisdom of God should be made known to the rulers and authorities in the heavenly realms" (3:10). For the manifold, multi-varied wisdom of God the *First Nations Version* has "like a rainbow with many colors." This is God's purpose and plan for the entire cosmos, and the "rulers and authorities" are system- and institution-influencing, hostile powers (cf. 2:1–2; 6:12), and that plan revolves around what God is doing in Christ Jesus "through the church" (3:11). As Barbara Brown Taylor once wrote, "The church's central task is an imaginative one. By that I do not mean a fanciful or fictional task, but one in which the human capacity to imagine—to form mental pictures of the self, the neighbor, the world, the future, to envision new realities—is both engaged and transformed" (Taylor, *Preaching Life*, 41). Our imaginations are truly set free when they are tethered to but one thing: the wisdom of God in Christ.

At times, I hear some Christian leaders yammer along about a claim that they are entering into their community to discern what God is doing in that location, and it all sounds just about right. Until one listens carefully to what is absent. Paul makes very clear *just exactly* what God is doing: revealing the multi-varied wisdom of God to the cosmic powers! How so?

1. What God is doing is in Jesus Christ.
2. What God is doing is embodied in the church.
3. What God is doing is drawing people to trust in Jesus.

4. What God is doing is granting humans, through Christ, direct access to God "with freedom and confidence" (3:12).

So, what we need to discern is how God is bringing people to himself through faith in Jesus Christ in local churches. Which means concentrating the local church on evangelism, on restoration of human relationships with God and with one another, on defeating evil, and on full access to this God in Christ. Which means liberating people from sin and systemic injustices and the empowering of people to have confidence in God.

Sadly, we are hearing more and more from those who have been lifelong church people coming to the realization that the "First" element of "in Christ" has become invisible. People come to church but are not hearing about and encountering Jesus (McKnight, Phillips, *Invisible Jesus*). If you have read Ephesians carefully you will have noticed how often Paul says, "in Christ." Forty-six times Paul mentions "Christ" and my count is that "in" is connected to Christ more than ten times already. Add a "with" or "under" Christ, and we get even more. Paul's core beliefs were Christ-haunted. To learn about God, go to Christ. To learn about your calling, go to Christ. To learn about salvation, go to Christ. To learn about the Christian way of life, go to Christ.

Christ at the center, the mystery of the gospel. Some of us have learned the famous morning prayer called "St. Patrick's Breastplate." I take this translation from *Celtic Daily Prayer* (347).

Christ be with me, Christ within me,
Christ behind me, Christ before me,
Christ beside me, Christ to win me,

Christ to comfort and restore me,
Christ beneath me, Christ above me,
Christ in quiet, Christ in danger,
Christ in hearts of all that love me,
Christ in mouth of friend and stranger.

God's grace comes to us in Christ, and it is embodied in a local church, the body of Christ in this world.

QUESTIONS FOR REFLECTION AND APPLICATION

1. How do unequal power dynamics keep churches from living out Paul's gospel?

2. Why would a multiethnic church need to be diverse in its leadership as well as its attendance?

3. Why does God give people gifts in the church?

4. What does Paul mean when he calls the gospel a mystery?

5. How does your church manifest the multi-varied wisdom of God in your community?

FOR FURTHER READING

Richard Bauckham, *The Blurred Cross: A Writer's Difficult Journey with God* (Grand Rapids: Baker Academic, 2024).

Celtic Daily Prayer, from the Northumbria Community (San Francisco: HarperSanFrancisco, 2002). I was moved to find my book's version of this prayer by Richard Bauckham's citation of it. The full version can be found here: https://en.wikipedia.org/wiki/Saint_Patrick's_Breastplate.

Dean Fleming, "Mission," in *The Dictionary of Paul and His Letters*, 2d ed. (Downers Grove: IVP Academic, 2023), 703–714.

Scot McKnight, Tommy Preson Phillips, *Invisible Jesus: A Book about Leaving the Church and Looking for Christ* (Grand Rapids: Zondervan Reflective, 2024).

Robert Chao Romero, Jeff M. Liou, *Christianity and Critical Race Theory: A Faithful and Constructive Conversation* (Grand Rapids: Baker Academic, 2023).

Barbara Brown Taylor, *The Preaching Life* (Cambridge: Cowley, 1993).

GRACE-SHAPED PRAYER

Ephesians 3:14–21

[14] *For this reason I kneel before [1] the Father,*

> [15] *[2] from whom every family in heaven and on earth derives its name.*
> [16] *[3] I pray that out of his glorious riches he may strengthen you with power through his Spirit in your inner being,*
> [17] *[4] so that Christ may dwell in your hearts through faith.*

> [3] *And I pray that you, being rooted and established in love, [18] may have power, together with all the Lord's holy people,*
>> *to grasp how wide and long and high and deep is the love of Christ,*
> [19] *and to know this love that surpasses knowledge—*
> [4] *that you may be filled to the measure of all the fullness of God.*

[20] *Now to him who is able to do immeasurably more than all we ask or imagine, according to his power that is at work within us,*

[21] *to him be glory in the church and in Christ Jesus throughout all generations, for ever and ever! Amen.*

[Reformatted. See below.]

Whether you dip into specific prayers in the Old Testament like Moses's petition about the people of Israel (Deuteronomy 9:26–29) or Solomon's uber-long petition (1 Kings 8), or in the New Testament like Jesus' prayer (John 17) or the early church's request (Acts 4:24–30), there are four or five basic elements to the prayers:

1. addressing God with a name (commonly Father)
2. rehearsing how God has acted in the past and thus reminding God
3. on the basis of what God has done in the past, asking God for what the person wants
4. expecting something to happen and,
5. mentioning one's access to God through the Lord Jesus Christ. The fifth element is a distinctive feature of the art of traditional, liturgical Christian prayers.

Here is a classic petition of the church, and these classic petitions are called "collects," and this is called the Collect for Purity (*Book of Common Prayer*, 355):

Almighty God,
to you all hearts are open, all desires known, and from you no secrets are hid:
cleanse the thoughts of our hearts by the inspiration of your Holy Spirit,
that we may perfectly love you, and worthily magnify your holy Name,

through Christ our Lord.
Amen.

A reverence formed, both in the Bible and in the church tradition, about how to speak to God when one is asking God for something. Instead of barging in with The Ask, the pray-er grew into a traditional model: how to address God with an appropriate biblical title and then to ponder God's actions in the past that correspond to the present request. Then the request is made, but it is made on the basis of God's former actions. The request is followed up with a commitment by the person to do something, or by a description of what God's action will bring about. Finally, the access to God in the Christian tradition makes clear that our only hope and foundation for God hearing and answering our petition is that we come to the Father through Jesus Christ (McKnight, *To You All Hearts*, 3–37).

Paul learned to pray like this at home and in synagogue formation. As a result of his Jesus-is-the-Messiah conversion, he adapted what he had learned. I have reformatted and marked today's reading with the numbers from the first paragraph to illustrate the prayer format. You can see that Paul doubles his request, and in the second major request for power, he doubles what this power can do: empower them to love and empower them to know that love (3:17–19). He finishes off the prayer in a typically Jewish manner, with a doxology (3:20–21). You and I may be tempted to think such a prayer is either too canned or that it can become a magical formula. Perhaps and perhaps, but this is the prayer tradition that formed over time in the pages of the Bible *on the basis of experiencing how to approach God reverently and honestly with our requests*. There is nothing bashful about these prayers, but there is nothing magical about them either. Sometimes the pray-er in the Bible jumps right into the request. Other times, as in today's reading, a traditional approach is noticeable.

Paul's God

Notice the first and second elements. Paul learned, from those who heard Jesus pray, to address God as Father (Luke 11:2; Matthew 11:25), which reveals God to be a loving father as well as the family's authority. The words that follow in Ephesians 3:15 clarify what Paul means by Father: this Father is the origin and source and relational connection for every "family" or "paternity" (*Second Testament*) in the universe. The *First Nations Version* translation approaches the single Greek term behind "family" from three angles: "all families, clans, and tribes." Paul's gospel of grace is a gospel that reaches all peoples because *the God of the gospel is the Father of all*. The prayer that follows flows from this understanding of God. The power and love and knowledge and indwelling Christ that come to expression in his petitions are designed to bring Jewish and gentile believers together into one family or, as Mitzi Smith expresses it, Paul believes in the "full enfranchisement of the Gentiles" (Smith, "Ephesians," 355).

Paul's Request

What pastor Paul wants for the Ephesians is densely expressed. The big idea is that he wants them to have the power of the Spirit, but he wants that power to flow directly from God's "splendorous wealth" and he wants this to happen in their innermost being (3:16; *Second Testament*). What Paul prayed for is what David de Silva calls an "experience . . . an encounter with divinity," the "invasion of our inmost selves by God's Holy Spirit, an invasion that would flood us with both power and a Person" so that God could do through us what God wants done among us (de Silva, *In Season*, 111–112). But the Spirit's empowering invasion is not the end, and we will look at the end in the fourth element immediately below. If it's not the end, the Spirit-in-us is the necessary beginning for the powerful transformation Paul has in mind for the Ephesians. De Silva genuinely asks, "Should we let him in?" If we do, he tells us, "He *will* mess with everything" (112).

Before we get there, I want to draw our attention to his second request, which he does not express until he says, "being rooted and established in love" (3:17). This may be their love for one another, or it may be God's love to them in Christ, that is, God's grace. He is here talking about their spiritual formation through instruction about God's love for them (1:4; 2:4; 3:17, 19; 5:2) that leads to their learning to love others (1:15; 4:2, 15, 16; 5:2; 6:23). Right here we might need to pause to catch the echo bounding from one city to another in the mission. Loving others is Paul's challenge for the diverse believers because crossing ethnic borders was as difficult then as it is now. Our Sunday morning ethnicity quotients are not unlike what at the time happened in Ephesus or Corinth.

Because the Ephesians have been taught this in their basic catechism, his prayer is that they will be empowered (by the Spirit) with all God's people "to grasp what is the width and length and height and depth" of Christ's love (3:17–18, *Second Testament*). Not only does he want them to "grasp" that love, he wants them to "know this love that surpasses knowledge" (3:19).

PAUL'S EXPECTATIONS

The goal or end of Paul's prayer is neither the empowerment of the Spirit nor is it grasping and knowing God's love. Both are of course very important, but Paul thinks like a mentor who wants the Ephesians to become spiritually mature. So, he has the "so that" lines [4]. He wants the Spirit to empower them "so that Christ may dwell in your hearts through faith" (3:17). That is, he prays ultimately that Christ will indwell them. Again, like St. Patrick's Breastplate mentioned previously (p. 55–56), he wants Christ in them and with them and before them and above them and next to them. And he wants God's power to work in them so they can grasp and know the love of Christ, but he wants this so "that you may be filled to the measure of all the fullness of God" (3:19). This fullness, Colossians will tell us, is Christ: "For in Christ all the fullness of the Deity lives in bodily form and in Christ you have been brought to fullness" (Colossians 2:9–10).

Paul's expectations then transcend Spirit-power and Spirit-knowing to become Christ-indwelling. His prayer for them is that they will become embodiments of Jesus himself.

PAUL'S DOXOLOGY

The benediction is probably one Paul partly learned in the synagogue and partly learned from other believers in Jesus and partly his own. At least "in Christ" sounds Pauline. Because benedictions occur at the end of many Sunday worship times, many have wondered if Paul was planning to end the letter right here. A scan of doxologies in the New Testament does not suggest they are suitable only for endings. When Kris and I listen to the preaching and teaching of my former high school track and field teammate, now a pastor in Dixon, Illinois, Mike Cole, we observe that at times he just pauses and gives God some glory. Paul does the same in his letters. Galatians has a doxology on the first page (1:3–5). Neither Romans 1:25 nor 9:4–5 nor 11:33–36 is at the end of the letter, and Paul's first letter to Timothy has a doxology early (1:17). When the Spirit prompts you to praise, you do so.

The collect tradition of the church closes with words about our access through Christ, while at least a later version of the Lord's Prayer* and this prayer in Ephesians 3 both end on a note of worship. The collects were designed for worship services, which meant the collect for the day did not require that kind of ending. Paul's does, and I believe we can learn from this. Like Jesus' prayer in Gethsemane, that request for the cup to pass him by that was followed with affirming whatever God's will is (Matthew 26:39), so Paul's prayer in Ephesians 3 is a request followed by a moment of surrendering worship. God, he says, can do "beyond all things uber-abundantly" (3:20; *Second Testament*), and God's power is "at work within us," so he praises God with "to him be glory in the church and in Christ Jesus throughout all generations, for ever and ever!" Those who heard those words affirmed them with a hearty "Amen!"

Far from the shore of the Ring of Kerry in the Republic of Ireland is an island. Tourists that we were and hearing that the weather was kind enough for a boat to take us out to Skellig Michael, we boarded for an adventure. Skellig Michael, a rocky place shooting straight out of the Atlantic with sheer cliffs, had been home for about a millennium for an edgy monastery of Celtic monks. My friend, Patrick Mitchel, knowing we had visited the island and enjoyed its abundance of puffins, recommended that I read Geoffrey Moorhouse's *Sun Dancing*. I marked these words as meaningful, words about and led by St. Fionán when they first landed on Skellig Michael: "Fionán did not even think about what he did next, for it was as natural to him as saying the

---

* The Lord's Prayer in Matthew ends on words that were almost certainly not original, but with words that were added as appropriate to ending the prayer. They are "for yours is the kingdom and the power and the glory forever. Amen."

Lord's prayer. He faced the distant land and the revealed power that now hung warmly over it, and raised his arms to the sky in gratitude. 'Glory to thee, thou glorious sun,' he began. His brothers stood around him, hands up turned in obeisance. 'Glory to thee, thou son,' they chorused. 'Face of the God of Life.' They said it so in the old tongue; and these were the first human voices ever raised in that place, where only birds and seals and the sacred elements had spoken before" (Moorhouse, *Sun Dancing*, 18). Then they climbed the steep cliff, a cliff with steps yet dangerous even today to ascend. We, too, made that ascent, doing our dead-serious best to avoid looking down the face of the cliff and hugging the inside of the destabilizing "stairs," and, once at the top, experienced what looked like an igloo of stone, the huts of the ancient monks of Skellig Michael. Where they praised God daily for centuries.

Celtic Christianity, only one of the many forms our faith has taken through the centuries, knows prayer, knows worship, knows severity, knows challenges, knows disciplines, knows joy, knows feasting, and knows that you and I can join them in their praise of the God of all creation.

QUESTIONS FOR REFLECTION AND APPLICATION

1. List two or three similarities in structure between prayers in the Old Testament and in the New Testament.

2. Why do you think traditional prayer models in the Bible and the church spend time reflecting on God's attributes and actions in the past?

3. What does Paul want God to do for the Ephesian Christians?

4. What has been your experience with written or formally formatted prayers? How do you like them in comparison with unscripted, spontaneous prayers?

5. Write a one-line benediction to give God glory right in the middle of your day. What do you want to express to God?

FOR FURTHER READING

David de Silva, *In Season and Out: Sermons for the Christian Year* (Bellingham, Washington: Lexham, 2019).

The Episcopal Church, *The Book of Common Prayer* (New York: Oxford, 1990).

Scot McKnight, *To You All Hearts Are Open: Revitalizing the Church's Pattern of Asking God* (Brewster, Massachusetts: Paraclete, 2021).

Geoffrey Moorhouse, *Sun Dancing: A Vision of Medieval Ireland* (San Diego: Harvest, 1997).

GRACE GIFTS UNIFY

Ephesians 4:1–16

[1] *As a prisoner for the Lord, then, I urge you to live a life worthy of the **calling** you have received.* [2] *Be completely humble and gentle; be patient, bearing with one another in love.* [3] *Make every effort to keep the **unity** of the Spirit through the bond of peace.* [4] *There is **one** body and **one** Spirit, just as you were called to **one** hope when you were called;* [5] ***one** Lord, **one** faith,* one *baptism;* [6] ***one** God and Father of all, who is over all and through all and in all.*

[7] *But to each one of us grace has been given as Christ apportioned it.* [8] *This is why it says:*

> *"When he ascended on high,*
> *he took many captives*
> *and gave gifts to his people."*

[9] *(What does "he ascended" mean except that he also descended to the lower, earthly regions?* [10] *He who descended is the very one who ascended higher than all the heavens, in order to fill the whole universe.)* [11] *So Christ himself gave the apostles, the prophets, the evangelists, the pastors and teachers,* [12] *to equip his people for works of service, so that the body of Christ may be built up* [13] *until we all*

*reach **unity** in the faith and in the knowledge of the Son of God and become mature, attaining to the whole measure of the fullness of Christ.*

*[14] Then we will no longer be infants, tossed back and forth by the waves, and blown here and there by every wind of teaching and by the cunning and craftiness of people in their deceitful scheming. [15] **Instead, speaking the truth in love, we will grow to become in every respect the mature body of him who is the head, that is, Christ. [16] From him the whole body, joined and held together by every supporting ligament, grows and builds itself up in love, as each part does its work.***

Recently I was asked to speak at a church celebrating the ordination of its pastor, Laura Tarro. When Laura asked me to speak, I had just finished teaching a class about "Pastor Peter," so my mind immediately went to 1 Peter 5's instructions about pastoring as mentoring. What the class did not attend to so much was that following Peter's wisdom for pastors the apostle turned to the entire congregation with more wisdom. Peter knew mentors and congregants would need to live up to each of their callings for the churches to flourish. So, the theme for my talk was this: "You will permit Pastor Laura to do what she is called to do *only* if you, Bethany Covenant, do what you are called to do." Maybe Peter got this idea from Paul!

What Paul no doubt faced was disunity in his churches, sometimes caused by bad ideas and other times by bad practices. Galatians and Romans both bring to the front ethnic and practical tensions between Jewish and gentile believers, Colossians informs us of some odd ideas about religious experiences, and the letters to the Corinthians take home the prize of problematic congregants and leaders. Ephesians doesn't tell us a word about what's going on in Ephesus that could have given Paul a reason to be so emphatic about unity. But we can assume disunity was a problem, regardless of the details. Lynn Cohick, drawing on her expertise in Roman and Greek social customs, draws our attention to the common quest for social honor and glory in that world—which could easily have been a source of disunity, and she points us to Acts 19:23–41's account of the social riot over Paul and the status, wealth, and prestige of the silversmith, Demetrius, as well as the honor to be reserved for the goddess Artemis. Unity of all, she observes, crashed into honor for the status-shaped and probably socially deserving.

THE CALLING IS UNITY

Paul's words would have been clearer than some in the church wanted them to be when he claimed that they were to "live a life worthy of the calling" (4:1), and immediately he makes it clear that "worthy" means "unity." The bold font words in the translation in our passage today express this calling to unity. Lynn Cohick concludes her discussion of this passage with, "Paul's defining message in this passage can be summarized in one word: one" (75). David de Silva complements Cohick when he suggests this passage presses us not to be "consumers" but "producers of unity" (de Silva, *In Season*, 203). The behaviors of verse two are the ingredients of verse three's "make every effort to keep the unity of the Spirit." Notice that the calling to unity is a calling to "keep" *what the Spirit has already created*: they are to keep "the Spirit's oneness" (4:3; *Second Testament*). We cannot create unity; we cannot make rules to establish unity. (We can try, but unity is the work of the Spirit in and through us.) A few academic books arrived on my doorstep recently, and one of the books had the title *Pneumaformity*, Mark Keown's word for the Spirit's power unleashed among us to transform us into looking more like Jesus Christ. Division reveals a lack of pneumaformity. The more Spirit, the more unity.

Paul turns now to two convictions about unity deriving from pneumaformity. The first is that everything that matters in the Faith is a one-thing:

One body,
One Spirit,
One hope,
One Lord,
One faith,
One baptism,
One God and Father.

I can't type those words without hearing John Michael Talbot sing them (Talbot, "One Faith"). Theologically, then, unity derives from a oneness of faith. We of course disagree about some topics, but what is held in common is sufficient for forming unity. Further, Paul believes the gifts of the Spirit will draw believers into mutual cooperation in the work of God (4:7–12) "until we all reach unity in the faith" (4:13). Notice, then, that verse fourteen is the negative of which verses fifteen and sixteen are the positive. The negative is childlikeness in the faith (4:14) while the maturity is unity, here expressed as love for one another that flows from mature union with Christ, who is the head, and the head unites (4:15–16). Please observe that headship here has nothing whatsoever to do with authority and everything to do with growing in unity. Christ is the "head," and it is "from him the whole body, *joined and held together by every supporting ligament, grows and builds itself up in love, as each part does its work*" (4:15–16). The unity of the Spirit is a unity that flows from the oneness themes of our faith, the exercise of our gifts, and our union with the Head, Christ.

71

THE SPIRIT UNITES

Let's take a brief, but closer, look at the Spirit as unifier. We are called to, among other things (1:3–14; 2:1–11; 3:7–13), a heartfelt commitment to keep, live by, and observe a Spirit-established unity, or "oneness" (4:3; *Second Testament*). The NIV's "unity" translates a Greek word that connects with the "one" words of 4:4–6. The Greek terms are *henotēs* and *hen*, which is why I prefer "oneness" instead of unity. In fact, oneness is a tighter-than-unity kind of unity. This oneness expresses also the "bond of peace" in the God-human and human-human relationships (4:3), with "bond" (*sundemos*) translating something that has been united by strapping, tying, gluing, tethering, knotting, bundling, or chaining tightly. This term ironically echoes the word "prisoner" in 4:1 (*desmios*). We commit ourselves to preserve what the Spirit has created: we are family, we are siblings, we are together.

The Spirit's illuminating of the church leads it to a oneness around seven fundamental confessions: One body (of Christ, the church of both Jews and gentiles), one Spirit, one hope (the kingdom of God where God is all in all), one Lord (Jesus Christ), one faith (allegiance to Christ), one baptism (in water), and one God and Father. The word Trinity is not used, but trinitarian thinking is clearly at work in this list. It is the misfortune of the church not to be able to live with the Spirit-led unity created by these fundamental truths. For sure, these seven truths morphed in adapting to new situations that led to the Nicene Creed, but that unity in the faith was shattered in the Reformation, leading to Protestant confessions and Catholic catechisms and then to today's silly local church attempts when a pastor himself attempts to articulate what that church needs to believe. If the beliefs and statements of faith do not *unite* in continuity with Ephesians 4:4–6, beware.

The Spirit's unifying work results in our loving one

another (4:2, 15), which empowers impoverishment, meekness, patience, and "truthing one another in love" (4:2, 15). Noticeably, Spirit-generated love for siblings in Christ turns us away from the destabilizing of false teachings which are "done by human 'rolling of the dice,' by trickery, in line with the device of deception" (4:14; *Second Testament*). Christian leaders, Christians, and Christian institutions turn from the Holy Spirit and toward the "device of deception" when branding and marketing mask truth-telling, when spin narrates the story instead of transparency, when those in power manipulate former words or even contracts to turn out the opposite of the promises, and when NDAs (non-disparagement agreements) cover up sins and behaviors that will harm the reputation of the leaders or institution.

THE SPIRIT UNITES THROUGH GIFTS

I return to the beginning when I urged Laura Tarro and Bethany Covenant to do what each is called to do so that they can work together for the gospel about Jesus Christ. What Peter talked about in 1 Peter 5 coheres in different terms with what Paul teaches in Ephesians 4:7–13: the Spirit-prompted gifts. Oneness flourishes through the Spirit-prompted gifts. As Esau McCaulley expresses it, "The common life . . . is possible because of the gifts of the Spirit" (McCaulley, "Ephesians," 427).

Paul presents the gifts of the Spirit here as:

1. graces that are given,
2. distributed to "each one of us"
3. by Christ who had ascended,
4. "for preparing the devoted ones" and "for service-works,"

5. for the formation of "the body of Christ," which
   gifts will be given to one another
6. until we arrive at the full oneness designed by
   God (combining NIV and *Second Testament*).

While the gifts Paul details here are "the apostles, the prophets, the evangelists, the teachers and pastors," which means his emphasis is on what we all perceive as platformed gifts, Paul explicitly says "to each one of us" at 4:7. Which means the list he gives in 1 Corinthians 12 is in mind at Ephesians 4:7 but gets narrowed in 4:11. But there's a way to see these four gifts that do not narrow. These platform-like gifts are designed "to equip" the congregations so the congregations can do "service-works" among themselves and in the community (4:11–12). Those service-works encompass the Spirit-prompted gifts in 1 Corinthians 12:28–30. We are unwise to think the New Testament provides an exhaustive list of the Spirit-prompted gifts, from which we are to find our own giftedness. Rather, think about how God uses you for others—that is where you will locate your gift. Teresa Morgan, an English priest (and professor), with a group around her, explored what it meant for every Christian to have a ministry. In her splendid little book, *Every-Person Ministry*, they came to this conclusion: "Gradually, we came to focus on five forms of ministry which we could all practise in and through our different occupations: love, listening, prophecy, reconciliation and teaching." But they noticed two more elements they all needed: "We also identified two things which might help us to minister better: dismantling the unhelpful passions in ourselves which stop us attending to others, and praying in ways which we could carry with us in our daily lives" (Morgan, *Every-Person Ministry*, 3). I find her approach very helpful.

What we all need to get is that in you being/doing who

God made you to be/do and me being/doing what God made me to be/do, we can realize we need one another to accomplish the bigger task than either of us! We can't achieve unity with one another until we realize each of us contributes and receives, and in receiving we admit our needs. Many of us would rather be consumers of others rather than givers, while others are givers but can't muster the courage to consume what others have to contribute to us. Both are needed for us to live as the body of Christ—the feet need the eyes, and the eyes need the arms.

In my lifetime Ephesians 4:11–13 has lifted its hand for far more attention than it has been given when it comes to healthy churches. The first was when Ray Stedman discovered what he called "body life" (Stedman, *Body Life*), and the second seems to have risen around Alan Hirsch (*The Forgotten Ways*). We can be grateful that both believe in the church, with Stedman especially emphasizing the importance of each person in a church discovering and exercising the gift God has given to them. The recent more quirky suggestion that the absence of the "APE" gifts in the church today, that is, apostles, prophets, evangelists is a major, if not the major, reason for the church's lack of flourishing today, and has led to an overemphasis on pastoring and teaching.[*] Unfortunately and detrimentally, apostle in this scheme too often becomes "entrepreneur" and prophet becomes a public, social critic. Both terms have been mismanaged routinely in the APE schemes. Ellen Davis, in her wonderful book on prophecy, writes, "Anything edgy is likely termed 'prophetic,' in a positive sense, as long as it makes no particular

---

[*] How should pastors and teachers be translated? I provide a wooden, literal translation so one can see what I'm talking about. Paul has *Christ gave the apostles, and the prophets, and the evangelists, and the pastors and teachers.* The explicit pattern of "the" before the gift is dropped for the last one because those two functions overlap in the gift of pastor-teacher.

reference to religious motivation or theological content." Her dual definition of a prophet strikes the bell for me: "They interpreted the faith for their time, and equally, they interpreted the times for the faithful" (Davis, *Biblical Prophecy*, xi, 3). Prophets interpret the times, but they do so with the ancient foundation: *Thus saith the Lord.*

While I value the importance of Spirit-based giftedness in each church, Ephesians 4 is not designed to provide some a magical, but forgotten, theory. I fear that the way many define these gifts lacks biblical rigor. In particular, a desire to anoint some today as apostles and prophets concerns me. By all means, we need to be open to the Spirit gifting each of us. Lynn Cohick delivers a serious alternative when she writes that Paul "is not describing gifts of leadership given to certain members of the body, nor is Paul establishing a specific church structure. . . . The emphasis is on the duties themselves (evangelizing, teaching, etc.), not on the people exercising the gift" (Cohick, Proclamation, 73). Thus, she claims these are resources Christ gives to the whole church. Her view is worthy of serious consideration.

In the USA today, in our conflicted political tensions, I'm far less concerned about debating the apostolic and prophetic gifts and far more concerned about our unleashing the Spirit to empower all in our churches to exercise how the Spirit wants to use them. Thus, that women would be released to use their gifts; that African Americans, Latin Americans, and Asian Americans would be given the freedom to use their gifts; that disabled people would be enabled by their gifts; that age discriminations of both young and old would end; and that gifts would not be sorted in our churches according to income and education and power and appearance. A fresh angle can be found in what Paul means by these gifts for the sake of the church in the *First Nations Version* of Ephesians 4:11: "He gifted us with message bearers, prophets, tellers of the good story, and wisdomkeepers, who watch over us like a shepherd watches over his sheep."

The church's unity has already been established by the Spirit. We can't create unity, no matter how hard we work at it. It's already there. We are called to live into it and to let it flow into us. But this much is also clear: Spirit-oneness will not be manifested in our churches today if each of us is not doing our part. That is, we each are gifted for the sake of the body of Christ, and we are summoned by this passage to exercise the grace-gift given to us by Christ.

QUESTIONS FOR REFLECTION AND APPLICATION

1. How might the cultural values of Paul's audience, like honor and status, have clashed with his value of unity?

2. Why do we need the Holy Spirit in order to achieve unity in the church?

3. What does it mean for Christ to be the "head" of this unity?

4. What role do spiritual gifts play in producing unity?

5. When you think about how God allows you to serve others, what does that show you about the gifts God has given you?

FOR FURTHER READING

Ellen F. Davis, *Biblical Prophecy: Perspectives for Christian Theology, Discipleship, and Ministry* (Louisville: Westminster John Knox, 2014).

David de Silva, *In Season and Out: Sermons for the Christian Year* (Bellingham, Washington: Lexham, 2019).

Alan Hirsch, *The Forgotten Ways: Reactivating Apostolic Movements* (2nd ed.; Grand Rapids: Brazos, 2016).

Mark J. Keown, *Pneumaformity: Transformation by the Spirit in Paul* (Grand Rapids: Kregel, 2024).

Teresa Morgan, *Every-Person Ministry: Reaching Out in Christ* (London: SPCK, 2011).

Ray Stedman, *Body Life* (rev. ed.; Grand Rapids: Discovery House, 1995). Originally published in 1972.

John Michael Talbot, "One Faith," Album: *The Regathering*, produced by Billy Ray Hearn and Rosasco, arranged by John Rosasco, featuring The London Philharmonic Orchestera and the Ambrosian Singers. Chatsworth, CA: Sparrow Records, 1988.

GRACE'S INERTIA FOR TRANSFORMATION

Ephesians 4:17–32

[17] *So I tell you this, and insist on it in the Lord, that you must no longer live as the Gentiles do, in the futility of their thinking.* [18] *They are darkened in their understanding and separated from the life of God because of the ignorance that is in them due to the hardening of their hearts.* [19] *Having lost all sensitivity, they have given themselves over to sensuality so as to indulge in every kind of impurity, and they are full of greed.*

[20] *That, however, is not the way of life you learned* [21] *when you heard about Christ and were taught in him in accordance with the truth that is in Jesus.* [22] *You were taught, with regard to your former way of life, to put off your old self, which is being corrupted by its deceitful desires;* [23] *to be made new in the attitude of your minds;* [24] *and to put on the new self, created to be like God in true righteousness and holiness.*

[25] *Therefore each of you must put off falsehood and speak truthfully to your neighbor, for we are all members of one body.* [26] *"In your anger do not sin": Do not let the sun go down while you are still angry,* [27] *and do not give the devil a foothold.* [28] *Anyone who has been stealing must steal no longer, but must work, doing something*

useful with their own hands, that they may have something to share with those in need.

29 Do not let any unwholesome talk come out of your mouths, but only what is helpful for building others up according to their needs, that it may benefit those who listen. 30 And do not grieve the Holy Spirit of God, with whom you were sealed for the day of redemption. 31 Get rid of all bitterness, rage and anger, brawling and slander, along with every form of malice. 32 Be kind and compassionate to one another, forgiving each other, just as in Christ God forgave you.

What *to do* uncovers what *not to do*. What not to do is always the flipside of what to do. People of genuine Christian character know the difference and consistently do what is right. Today's reading reveals the back-and-forth of an apostle who has watched new believers and new churches form from a former way of life into a new way of life. Our passage contains lots of Don'ts and Do's (McKnight, *Fellowship*, 120–122), but they are more than lists. The path from their past to the present was not easy for the Ephesians, and to whomever this letter was sent, nor was it easy for Paul or his co-workers. What Paul has learned is that grace, giving it sufficient time, renews and transforms a person's life. The back-and-forths of today's reading reminded the first century's and today's audiences of their pre-conversion life and of their new life in Christ. We dare not reduce the gospel response to accepting Jesus into our hearts and then going to heaven when we die. The gospel of God's grace transforms because grace, as was detailed in today's reading, is efficacious. Grace glues us to God in Christ, and God's Spirit indwells us, and where the Spirit of the Lord is there is the freedom of renewal and holiness (2 Corinthians 3:17).

I stand with David de Silva who, in his book *Transformation*, exhorts us to wrestle with this definition of the gospel and its impact:

> God offers you the means to be reconciled with him and to become a new person who will want and love and do what is pleasing to him because the Spirit of his Son will live in you and *change* you. The result of God's kindness and activity is that you will live a new kind of life now and, after death, live forever with him. (de Silva, *Transformation*, 2)

Paul does not believe total transformation happens within the first hour. But what he does believe is that the Lord of the gospel effectively works in us, that the Father of the gospel of grace loves us into change, and that the Spirit of the gospel of grace empowers us to change. To the above quotation from de Silva I add this one, which is a bit longer:

> I am reminded of something presented in many seventh- or eighth-grade science classes, namely the concept of inertia, which states that an object in motion tends to remain in motion at the same speed and in the same direction unless acted on by an imbalanced force. Our self-centered cravings and agendas kept us moving in a particular direction, but the cross of Jesus has the power to stop us in our tracks—as it did to Paul himself. Such a display of selflessness, of God-centeredness and other-centeredness, at the very least *has* to slow us down in our self-centered trajectory. And God's gift of the Holy Spirit introduces into our lives an imbalanced force, of force for which sin and self-centeredness are no equals, freeing us from the inertia in, in effect, of the impulses of what Paul often calls our "former self," our

"old self"—the "self" from which God saved us, because its end is the accumulation of a pile of injustices, harm to others, and condemnation for the failure to discover and live out God's purposes for the person God created. (de Silva, *Transformation*, 49)

Today's reading reveals the former inertia and the Holy Spirit's power to effect a new life. In a word, transformation. In a few more words, Paul believed being a Christian would make a noticeable difference in a person's life.

SIN'S INERTIA

In reading this passage today we can discover the tragic inertia of sin by marking each sin mentioned. Here goes, and all these are found in the printed passage above, so I will not use quotation marks for each: futility of their thinking, darkened in their understanding, separated from the life of God, ignorance resulting from the hardening of their hearts, the loss of sensitivity, sensuality, indulgences, impurity, greed, the old self, deceitful desires, falsehood, the devil's foothold, stealing, unwholesome talk, grieving the Holy Spirit of God, bitterness, rage and anger, brawling and slander, every form of malice. That's quite a list, don't you agree? These sins connect to worldview (thinking, understanding, ignorance), relationships, the heart, desires, finances, what we say, and to interpersonal sins. These sins describe how believers used to "walk around" in their pre-Jesus days (4:17; *Second Testament*; cf. 4:1). Cohick explains the connections at work in these words: "The behavior is habitual, with the pitiless downward spiral of darkened mindset producing self-centered, immoral behavior, which hardens the heart, leading to more darkness and additional sin and futility. And this behavior harms others; greed takes from neighbors, and sexual excesses are gratified by slaves or those of lower social status. Paul does not excuse such behavior on account of the perpetrator's ignorance of God" (Cohick, Proclamation, 83).

A List of 20 Sins and Sinful Conditions

1. futility of their thinking,
2. darkened in their understanding,
3. separated from the life of God,
4. ignorance resulting from the hardening of their hearts,
5. the loss of sensitivity,
6. sensuality,
7. indulgences,
8. impurity,
9. greed,
10. the old self,
11. deceitful desires,
12. falsehood,
13. the devil's foothold,
14. stealing,
15. unwholesome talk,
16. grieving the Holy Spirit of God,
17. bitterness,
18. rage and anger,
19. brawling and slander,
20. every form of malice.

To be frank, Paul's hard on the Ephesians. Some of them may have muttered *We weren't that bad*. He might counter with, but those who encounter the holiness of God perceive sin for what it really is, regardless of how it is explained by others; those who experience the love of God come to terms with their former treatment of others; those who are ravished by the grace of God realize how unworthy they were (and are) of God's grace; those who observe the workings of the Spirit's transforming powers in their present life become aware of how impossible a Spirit-shaped life was in their former days, and those who come to know the sweetness of Christ wonder how they ever could have not loved and trusted and followed him. Vibrating just below the surface in this listing of sins is the tension that exists between people of different ethnicities, which for Paul was between believers with a Jewish or a gentile heritage. Some of these sins, in other words, revealed communal strife, ghosting, gaslighting, and even redlining on the basis of stereotypes of ethnicities.

Paul's descriptions of the past of these believers are only accurate because of where Paul now stands—in a place far removed from where he used to be. Converts to Jesus often form what is called an "anti-rhetoric" about their past, and that's what Paul is doing for the gentile converts in Ephesus. The longer he lived the more perceptive he became about his and their former sinfulness. It is a fact that humans struggle like caged animals when they begin to confront their sinfulness, and some struggle for a long time. But once they give in, and once the Spirit begins to work, the former sins become all too obvious and a confession of those sins easy. I believe the tradition of the church for a time of confession each Sunday morning wisely reminds us of God's grace but also prompts reflection, admission, and gratitude for what God has done, is doing, and will do in my life.

But sin fights back. De Silva's idea of sin's inertia helps us to pin that inertia on the flesh or the NIV's "your former way of life . . . [and] your old self" or *The Second Testament's* "former behavior [and] the ancient human" (4:22). The flesh is with us till we die; the old self remains till we die. But the flesh loses its voice, and its former ruling commands become little more than whispers we barely hear.

A light example. When I was a teenager, I could sleep and sleep and sleep, till 10:00 AM or later at times. I no longer not only do not "sleep in" but I have no desire, no temptation, no possibility of even wanting to stay in bed past 6:00 AM, and 5:30 AM has become a late start to my day. Okay, we are officially just over the line of seventy years old, but you get the point. What drove the old (but young) days is no longer a desire in the new (and senior) days.

GRACE'S INERTIA

Christian ethics are not to be shaped by the negatives, by what we are not to do, but by the positives, what we are to do. The Ephesians have been "apprenticed to Christos," or they learned Christ, and it was not in the way of their past behaviors (4:20; *Second Testament*). The text is more direct than the NIV's "way of life you learned when you heard about Christ" (4:20–21). In fact, Christ is the object of the verb "apprenticed" or "learned," so it is not that they learned "about" Christ but that they were apprenticed to him or learned him (as a person). Mark Roberts is right, commenting that "but the awkward bluntness of learned Christ . . . underscores the fact that Christianity is focused in a person." He continues with "The essence of the Christian life is not a moral system constructed by a fine moral teacher. Rather, it is life in Christ: trusting him, knowing him, following him, loving him, being created anew in him, learning from him, imitating him, sharing in his work" (Roberts, *Ephesians*, 150). Learning Christ breaks down sin's inertia. By the way, a brief sketch of what early Christian discipleship may have looked like can be found in Ephesians 4:22–24.

The "imbalanced force" (de Silva above) of the gospel

stopped us in our tracks and propelled us over time to change our course, and over time the inertia of grace began to control the direction of our lives. Paul's tall pile of words about this change of directions looks like this:

A Glimpse of a Life Redirected

1. put off your old self . . .
2. put on the new self,
3. made new in the attitude of your minds,
4. created to be like God,
5. true righteousness,
6. holiness,
7. put off falsehood,
8. speak truthfully,
9. (and talking about sleeping) do not let the sun go down while you are still angry,
10. stealing no longer,
11. working with one's hands,
12. sharing with those in need,
13. no unwholesome talk,
14. speaking what is helpful,
15. benefiting those who hear us,
16. not grieving the Holy Spirit,
17. getting rid of bitterness,
18. rage and anger,
19. brawling and slander and malice,
20. and becoming kind
21. and compassionate and forgiving.

In the middle of this (v. 24), Paul instructs the Ephesians "to be like God"! Quite the order. But humans are made in

God's image, the renewal of the Spirit makes us like Christ, and Christ is the perfect image of God (Colossians 3:10)—so God-likeness, or its abbreviation "godliness," is appropriate. Again, these are the virtues of a new worldview and mindset, a new heart, a new set of behaviors that measure up well with the will of God, transparency and integrity in speech, learning new emotions, boundaries on the possessions of others, peaceful relations, generosity, and God-shaped grace-giving to others. The last verse reads, "Be gracious to one another, commiserating, gracing one another just as God has graced you in Christos" (Ephesians 4:32; *Second Testament*).

Sin's inertia, by the power of the Spirit, is replaced by grace's inertia, which (as just mentioned) propels us over time in a new direction. We are headed for the kingdom of God where sin is banished, where systemic evil is erased, and where love and systemic justice and goodness and peace are established, flourishing, and amazingly growing better each and every day throughout all eternity. The inertia of grace does all that and more, and all this is beyond our comprehension in the here and now. We are responsible for choosing to surrender to grace, to give in to the Spirit's work, and to put off the old life. As *First Nations Version* expresses it, "Take off that worn-out and stained outfit of your past life" (4:22).

Mitzi Smith observes that among her own people, African Americans, a socio-economic class consciousness can form. So, she writes, "too many Africana people have obtained middle-class and upper-middle-class status; moved into more affluent neighborhoods, taking our tax dollars with us; enrolled our children in more financially sound school districts; attended churches in the neighborhoods we left behind; and yet become uncomfortable should people from the communities we abandoned dare to sit next to us in our pews. Too many of us are leaving, never to glance back" (Smith, "Ephesians–2 ed.," 379). The Ephesians may have done the same on the people of their past, and they may be doing the same with their own fellow believers, and these leavings are not the design of the gospel. They abandoned their past but in so doing abandoned the people of their past. In their wonderful new study of pastors of color who pastor multiracial churches, Korie Little and Rebecca Kim map the life story of these pastors: they were mostly nurtured in their own ethnoracial churches, were educated in white establishment universities, colleges, and seminaries where they imbibed white culture, and then discovered they no longer "fit" in their former ethnoracial churches, so they have moved into the pioneering of multiracial churches. Their book concentrates on the importance of pioneering, but the stories of these pastors being estranged from their former communities echoes how change in life can lead us away from our only true home (Edwards and Kim, *Estranged Pioneers*). These contemporary examples of creating estrangement from one's home community help us understand what was happening among the Ephesians when they failed to remember that God's grace transforms, but it does not create class consciousness in its wake.

Those who knew the apostle John in his youthful days of discipleship knew he had a nasty, vindictive desire to toss Sodom and Gomorrah's fires onto the Samaritans because they did not receive their preaching about Jesus (Luke 9:51–55). But those who knew him late in life called him the apostle of love (1 John). Grace's inertia transforms. Those who knew Paul in Tarsus or in his salad days of becoming a rabbi in Jerusalem, under the great Gamaliel, knew he was a hot-headed zealot who despised and sought to destroy the sect of those following Jesus (Galatians 1:13–14). But those from Tarsus or Jerusalem who met Paul after decades of mission work among the gentiles would have called him the apostle of grace. It takes time, but the inertia of grace effects transformation.

The face of grace, which the Ephesians learned, is Jesus himself. I join with a brief section of the Caedmon of Whitby traditional prayer (*Celtic Daily Prayer*, 201):

I have a dream
that all the world will meet You,
and know You, Jesus,
in Your living power,
that someday soon
all people everywhere will hear Your story
and hear it in a way they understand.

So many who have heard
    Forget to tell the story.

Here am I, Jesus:
    Teach me.

Special Note to the Reader: To cut Ephesians into sections will inevitably run into a problem for this series. Today's passage runs from 4:17 all the way to (at least) 5:20, if not 6:9 or 6:20! We divide today's reading from the next one to make each passage more manageable for a day's reflection.

QUESTIONS FOR REFLECTION AND APPLICATION

1. What roles do the Father, Son, and Holy Spirit each play in transforming Christians?

2. How does the inertia of sin effect a human life?

3. By contrast, how does the inertia of grace effect a human life?

4. What are some differences between living in a moral system with Jesus as the moral leader and life in Christ?

5. What noticeable difference does being a Christian make in your life?

FOR FURTHER READING

Celtic Daily Prayer, from the Northumbria Community (San Francisco: HarperSanFrancisco, 2002).
Korie Little Edwards, Rebecca Y. Kim, *Estranged Pioneers: Race, Faith, and Leadership in a Diverse World* (New York: Oxford, 2024).

Scot McKnight, *A Fellowship of Differents: Showing the World God's Design for Life Together* (Grand Rapids: Zondervan, 2014).

David de Silva, *Transformation: The Heart of Paul's Gospel* (Bellingham, Washington: Lexham, 2014).

THE SPIRIT OF GRACE

Ephesians 5:1–20

[1] *Follow God's example, therefore, as dearly loved children* [2] *and walk in the way of love, just as Christ loved us and gave himself up for us as a fragrant offering and sacrifice to God.*

[3] *But among you there must not be even a hint of sexual immorality, or of any kind of impurity, or of greed, because these are improper for God's holy people.* [4] *Nor should there be obscenity, foolish talk or coarse joking, which are out of place, but rather thanksgiving.* [5] *For of this you can be sure: No immoral, impure or greedy person—such a person is an idolater—has any inheritance in the kingdom of Christ and of God.* [6] *Let no one deceive you with empty words, for because of such things God's wrath comes on those who are disobedient.* [7] *Therefore do not be partners with them.*

[8] *For you were once darkness, but now you are light in the Lord. Live as children of light* [9] *(for the fruit of the light consists in all goodness, righteousness and truth)* [10] *and find out what pleases the Lord.* [11] *Have nothing to do with the fruitless deeds of darkness, but rather expose them.* [12] *It is shameful even to mention what the disobedient do in secret.* [13] *But everything exposed by the light becomes visible—and everything that is illuminated becomes a light.*

[14] *This is why it is said:*

> *"Wake up, sleeper,*
> *rise from the dead,*
> *and Christ will shine on you."*

[15] *Be very careful, then, how you live—not as unwise but as wise,* [16] *making the most of every opportunity, because the days are evil.* [17] *Therefore do not be foolish, but understand what the Lord's will is.* [18] *Do not get drunk on wine, which leads to debauchery. Instead, be filled with the Spirit,* [19] *speaking to one another with psalms, hymns, and songs from the Spirit. Sing and make music from your heart to the Lord,* [20] *always giving thanks to God the Father for everything, in the name of our Lord Jesus Christ.*

Transformed Christian behaviors were called into question because they came into play on Day One for the new converts in the early church. When the apostle Paul began planting churches in Asia Minor and Greece, he quickly learned the importance of grace and forgiveness, of grace and transformation, and as a leader, of grace and patience. Gentiles had not been trained in the covenant with Abraham or in the law of Moses. So, Paul had to figure out how best to teach gentiles what it meant to be a follower of Jesus. Following Jesus, of course, meant living in the Story that began with Abraham and Moses. Today's passage opens a window on what it was like to teach gentiles how to live like Christ.

TWO APPROACHES

Ethics were often taught in one of two ways: mastering the particulars, which in the case of the Pentateuch meant some 616 commands or prohibitions. Nearly all of these became so instinctual for Jews that one learned them in the home and in one's community in childhood and early adult years.

The other way to teach ethics is to reduce them to a singular theme that can explain all the particulars. A scholar of the law, who knew contemporary discussions about the matter, asked Jesus which of all the commands was the greatest. Jesus pointed to two commands in the law of Moses and glued them together: love God and love others as yourself (Mark 12:28–34). From Jesus Paul himself picked up on the centrality of love (Galatians 5:14; Romans 13:9). So, too, did James (2:8) and clearly John couldn't write a sentence without somehow including love (1 John).

Reduction answered the most common question of new believers about how best to live in the way of Jesus. The answers of early Christian teachers sometimes varied, but reductions remained. While I believe Paul borrowed from Jesus, one of his most important reductions can be found at the end of today's reading. The answer to the question about the best way to live is "be filled with the Spirit" (Ephesians 5:18). Therein lies a personal story for me. I grew up in American fundamentalism of a Baptist variety. As a six-year-old I prayed to receive Jesus into my heart and so was assured I was going to heaven if I were to die. Preaching and Sunday School lessons, not to ignore Awana ministries and Sunday evening's "Sparks" before the Sunday evening service—in each of these, death and facing the judgment were a constant. A few years after my Sinner's Prayer moment, I was baptized, having gone through a basic doctrinal survey class. I do not now know my spiritual condition in those years, but what I did come to realize was that I was definitely out of sorts with God, with my church, and in my innermost soul. So, at seventeen I went to a Christian summer camp in Iowa where my life was changed. That week's emphasis was the fruit of the Spirit, and the foundation for those fruits forming in us was to be filled with the Spirit. Before breakfast—I was always an early riser—I wandered down to an area where we had evening sessions, I sat down under a tree, and I prayed, "Father, forgive me of my sins and fill me with your Spirit." It happened. I didn't speak in tongues, and I didn't suddenly burst into uttering prophetic words, but my entire inner being came alive, and from that day I wanted to live as a Christian. I was a Spirit-drenched follower of Jesus. I devoted myself to daily Bible reading and began to pursue the vocation of being a professor. Here I am more than fifty years later, doing what I wanted to become at that time.

If I am asked how Paul understood the Christian life, I will nearly always reduce it to: Be filled with the Spirit. If one lives the Spirit-filled life, one will do all God wants. Every Do and every Don't in these passages can be done or not done as God wants *only if one is filled with the Spirit*. For some "be filled with the Spirit" is a bit too ambiguous, mystical, or subjective. I don't agree, but for such persons, Paul's Do's and Don'ts are very good indicators of what a Spirit-filled person's behaviors look like. Even if Paul can reduce the Christian life to the Spirit-filled life, he's not bashful about giving some particulars. Four of which are found in today's reading.

LOVE

Live like God, in 4:24 and 5:1, is both a profound theological truth and a portal to verse two where living like God means walking in the way of love. The theological truth is that Who God is forms Ultimate Truth and Reality—all caps because that's how important that theological truth is. If God is holy, holiness is the ultimate truth and reality. If God is love, love is the ultimate truth and reality. God is love (1 John 4:8, 16). So, "be copies of God" (Ephesians 5:1; *Second Testament*) is tied immediately to "as loved children" and to "walk around in love" as Jesus has loved us, and his love is seen in having sacrificed himself for us (5:2). God-like love is to offer oneself to God and to another. Love is the first fruit of the Spirit (Galatians 5:22) so those who are filled with the Spirit love God, love themselves, and love others. Esau McCaulley rightly reminds us that "It is important here to note who exactly functions as a model for human behavior . . . it is God and his Son whose sacrifice for us that points the way" (McCaulley, "Ephesians," 431). He then connects this God-likeness, not human-likeness, to avoiding thinking of any particular culture as the true model for the Christian life. I have myself lived for a significant time in both the USA and in Europe (England), and church here is not church there. (Even if Americans are doing their best to export their church models, preaching styles, size of churches, and measurements of success to Europe.) Hispanic, Asian, and African American Christians today often learn the "proper" and "best" way to do church from white American Christianity and Christian leaders. But God, not white Americans, is the model for behavior.

As I have often clarified in various books in this *Everyday Bible Studies* series, love is a rugged, affective commitment to be with someone, to be for someone, and to be in the process of mutual growth in Christoformity—and now we can add "in Pneumaformity." Love is not reducible to the sensation that we feel when we know we are loved, but deep love is filled with sensations and feelings. Love's sensations shape us into people who, out of a commitment to others, want to be present with them, want to become an advocate for their good, and want to grow with them in imitating God's love for others.

SEX, MONEY, SPEECH

By far the two most common problems, especially for Jewish Christian leaders in the early church, because of the number of gentile conversions, were (1) idolatries and (2) sexual immoralities. Read Romans 1:18–32 or 1 Corinthians 5 and 8. There you will meet up with the problems these early churches faced on a daily basis. In the second section of today's reading (Ephesians 5:3–7) we encounter the stereotypical sins of gentiles. Paul does not limit it to those two famous sins, but they make their appearances (5:3, 5). A typical, if also stereotypical, Roman (and Greek) male was known for sexual procreative relations with his wife and sexual recreational relations with slaves and prostitutes. Which is why for many males, conversion was either a bridge too far or one they'd like to retrace. In fact, the NIV translates two different terms with the word "immoral" (5:3 [*porneia*], 5), but verse five has a word that is probably better translated "prostituting" or visiting a prostitute (*pornos*).

Paul mixes into the problems with sexual immorality the challenge of "greed" (5:3, 5), which Paul connects to idolatry—so connected, he can say greed is idolatry (5:5). Greed is "wanting-more-and-more" (*Second Testament*) because it is driven by desire and stimulations and acquisitions, and along with those, a cheap status elevation comes with lots of possessions. Lynn Cohick's words might stop us in our tracks: "Greed is something easily seen in others, but rarely viewed in oneself" (Cohick, Proclamation, 93). Ouch. Or, take some medicine from Dorothy Sayers in her incomparable novel, *Gaudy Night*: "as any student of literature must, she knew all the sins of the world by name, but it was doubtful whether she recognized them when she met them in real life" (Sayers, *Gaudy Night*, 16).

There is another side to the issue of money and greed—some want more and more, some hoard it, while others think too much about it but are secretive. Elizabeth Strout, in her wonderful novel *Abide With Me*, writes about this tendency: "many people, particularly Protestants whose ancestors had come from puritan stock and had been living up in New England for many, many years, held an attitude toward money that had wrapped around it some cloak of unsavoury secrecy. The less spent, the better. The less talked about, better still. It was a bit like food: there to sustain you but not, past a certain point, to be fully enjoyed. That was gluttony" (Strout, *Abide With Me*, 123). A Spirit-filled Christian does not engage in illegitimate sexual relations, nor is he or she driven or obsessed by wealth and possessions. The Spirit forms people into holiness, transparency, and generosity.

Knowing that churches were filled with sinful people, and knowing that church folks talk at times in unwholesome ways, Paul instructs them that a Spirit-filled person avoids "obscenity, foolish talk or coarse joking" and then a few verses later adds "empty words" (5:4, 6). The *First Nations Version* connects this coarse talk to sexual talk: "sexual relations should be spoken of with respect—no foolish talk or dirty jokes. Instead, give thanks *for this sacred gift of creating new life.*" Others connect this language to social status. Thus, labeling, denigrating, deceiving, false narrating, gaslighting, and personal insulting are "not proper" (*Second Testament*) because, for the Spirit-filled person, what is proper is uttering thanksgivings (5:4). Paul was not Pollyannaish about this, however, for he too could label people and speak harshly when he thought the gospel was at stake (cf. Galatians 2:11–14; 2 Corinthians 10–13; 1 Timothy 1:19–20).

What might surprise us today is how serious Paul is about these matters. It's one thing to say something is "out of place" (5:4), but Paul contends the sexually immoral and greedy will not obtain "any inheritance in the kingdom of Christ and of God" (5:5), and that those with filthy degrading speech are the reasons for "God's wrath" (5:6). One rhetorical method to grab the attention of your intended audience is to threaten with the ultimate punishment. Jesus and the apostles both threatened audiences with final judgment, and while Jonathan Edwards has been America's favorite bad example of this, the history of the church is filled with preachers threatening their audiences. I believe in the final judgment; I also believe the threat ought to be rare and used with pastoral sensitivities. Tone matters in how we speak about such topics. I like how Lynn Cohick enters into the tone of Paul: "we don't need to hear a thunderous voice behind these words, but perhaps those of a gentle, wise elder who has seen much sin and wants his congregation to live in the light that is theirs through Christ" (Cohick, Proclamation, 95–96).

LIGHT AND DARKNESS

Morality has often been taught with the images of darkness (bad) and light (good). Once I was preaching on the contrast between darkness and light, which easily slides (and my sermon slid) into black and white. After the service, a white man approached me and asked me to reconsider my language because those born with dark skin could easily have heard what I said as degrading Blackness. He was right, and I have never read the contrast of darkness and light without thinking of his kind admonition. When reading commentaries by our dark-skinned brothers and sisters, I am surprised that there are not more warnings about the dangers of this language. I raise the matter for your consideration. Are we using the language of light and darkness in ways that are insensitive to persons of color?

The metaphors are designed to warn the audiences of the Do's and Don'ts, of sins and the ways of God, and what it means to live in the flesh or to be filled with the Spirit. Formerly the Ephesians were in darkness, but "you are now light in the Lord" (5:8), and to live as the light is to practice "goodness, righteousness and truth" and learning to please the Lord (5:9–10). What occurs in that darkness is so shameful Paul avoids detailing the depths of the sins, and so he calls the Ephesians, by quoting from an unidentifiable source but probably an early Christian hymn, to wake up and to rise from the dead and "Christ will shine on you" (5:14). This quotation suggests that Christ's shining on us makes us lights in this world, and many think this could have been sung when new believers were baptized.

WISDOM, WINE, SPIRIT

Another reduction occurs. This time it's wisdom, and we would be wise to connect this wisdom with the light and evil, unwise, and foolishness with the metaphor of darkness (5:15–17). As Eugene Peterson once preached, "Wisdom is the skilled living of truth in everyday reality. . . . Wisdom is God's Spirit working within us to fashion our lives into wholeness in the actual environment in which we find ourselves: in these circumstances, in this neighborhood, in this family" (Peterson, *As Kingfishers Catch Fire*, 196). Marilynne Robinson, in an almost throwaway line, said, "wisdom, which is almost always another name for humility" (Robinson, *When I Was a Child I Read Books*, 27), and if anything speaks of wisdom it is enough humility to perceive what the Spirit is telling us, to do what the Spirit wants, and to do so when the Spirit wants.

To be alert enough to discern the wise from the foolish, the light from the darkness, Paul urges them not to "booze it up with wine" but instead to be "filled up in Spirit" (5:18, *Second Testament*). A Spirit-filled person turns from obscenities and coarse language to "speaking to yourselves in string-accompanied songs and hymns and spiritual odes, singing and playing the strings in your heart to the Lord" (5:19, *Second Testament*). Here is an indicator that some brought

101

their musical instruments into the gatherings of believers. What surprises is that these songs are how the believers were to speak *amongst themselves.* Now I'm not the only person who doubts they were being instructed to talk to one another by quoting or singing hymns or songs—like "You Say" by Lauren Daigle or "How Great Is Our God" by Chris Tomlin. Rather, Paul urges them to turn from coarse talk to ChristianSpeak, which involves praising God together and giving thanks to God, and "thanksgiving" is a word built on grace (*eucharisteō*).

Because the next passage jumps up and down with so much heated controversy, something needs to come to the surface here: giving thanks (v. 20) is a participle that parallels in structure the participle translated as a verb in the NIV with "Submit" (v. 21). The *Second Testament* ends verse 20 with a comma and then translates "ordering yourselves under one another in awe of Christos" (5:21). There is neither a major section break, as my copy of the NIV has it ("Instructions for Christian Households"), nor a shift from a participle to a main verb, and neither is the main verb an imperative as the NIV has it ("Submit" is an imperative). So, I reproduce for emphasis how I translated the passage to prepare us for the next reading.

Verse 20: always thanking for everything (in our Lord Yēsous Christos's name) the Father-God,
Verse 21: ordering yourselves under one another in awe of Christos . . .

QUESTIONS FOR REFLECTION AND APPLICATION

1. Why do you think Paul reduces his understanding of the Christian life to "Be filled with the Spirit"?

2. What are some of the observable evidences that a person is filled with the Spirit?

3. Consider the common sins Paul points to as evidence of a lack of Spirit-filling in a person in Ephesus. How are they different from or similar to common sins today?

4. Look at your life and your own personal common sins. Where do you see evidence of the Spirit at work in you, transforming you?

5. How would you like to change your speech this week, orienting yourself more toward giving thanks to God and loving people?

FOR FURTHER READING

Eugene Peterson, *As Kingfishers Catch Fire: A Conversation on the Ways of God Formed by the Words of God* (Colorado Springs: Waterbrook, 2017).

Marilynne Robinson, *When I Was a Child I Read Books: Essays* (New York: Farrar, Staus and Giroux, 2012).

Dorothy Sayers, *Gaudy Night* (New York: Harper & Row, 1986).

Elizabeth Strout, *Abide with Me* (New York: Random House, 2006).

GRACE IN THE HOUSEHOLD

Ephesians 5:21–6:9

²¹ Submit to one another out of reverence for Christ.

²² Wives, submit yourselves to your own husbands as you do to the Lord. ²³ For the husband is the head of the wife as Christ is the head of the church, his body, of which he is the Savior. ²⁴ Now as the church submits to Christ, so also wives should submit to their husbands in everything.

²⁵ Husbands, love your wives, just as Christ loved the church and gave himself up for her ²⁶ to make her holy, cleansing her by the washing with water through the word, ²⁷ and to present her to himself as a radiant church, without stain or wrinkle or any other blemish, but holy and blameless. ²⁸ In this same way, husbands ought to love their wives as their own bodies. He who loves his wife loves himself. ²⁹ After all, no one ever hated their own body, but they feed and care for their body, just as Christ does the church—³⁰ for we are members of his body. ³¹ "For this reason a man will leave his father and mother and be united to his wife, and the two will become one flesh." ³² This is a profound mystery—but I am talking about Christ and the church. ³³ However, each one of you also must love his wife as he loves himself, and the wife must respect her husband.

⁶:¹ Children, obey your parents in the Lord, for this is right.

[2] *"Honor your father and mother"—which is the first command-ment with a promise—*[3] *"so that it may go well with you and that you may enjoy long life on the earth."*

[4] *Fathers, do not exasperate your children; instead, bring them up in the training and instruction of the Lord.*

[5] *Slaves, obey your earthly masters with respect and fear, and with sincerity of heart, just as you would obey Christ.* [6] *Obey them not only to win their favor when their eye is on you, but as slaves of Christ, doing the will of God from your heart.* [7] *Serve whole-heartedly, as if you were serving the Lord, not people,* [8] *because you know that the Lord will reward each one for whatever good they do, whether they are slave or free.*

[9] *And masters, treat your slaves in the same way. Do not threaten them, since you know that he who is both their Master and yours is in heaven, and there is no favoritism with him.*

If the gospel put serious challenges to new believers about such matters as sexual relations, speech, where to worship and whom to worship, as well as money, what happens to the home when grace enters? Once again, we can sort today's reading out by turning it all into Do's and Don'ts at Home: Wives, do this; husbands, do that, etc. But this approach again will fail the larger picture Paul is painting before the Christians of western Asia Minor (modern Turkey) of what a Spirit-filled house looks like.

Wives and husbands, children and fathers, as well as slaves and masters began asking on Day One of Christian living what the gospel had to do with relationships in the household. As Esau McCaulley helpfully states it, Paul "was trying to articulate the ways in which the gospel reorders all relational interactions, often with extended concern for those most at risk"—wives, children, the enslaved (McCaulley, "Ephesians," 432). The various traditional (for Greece and Rome) statuses Paul brings up here, we need to remind ourselves, are not distant and abstract categories discussed by social thinkers. Think of one home or villa in Ephesus, think of one head of the household (the father, only perhaps the mother), and think of all these others as connected to that household—these status markers of the Greek world of Ephesus had names and faces attached to them. Each Ephesian muttered *that's me* when their category was named. Each was a personality, a character, a vibrant human.

Furthermore, the larger context in Ephesians has led us to see three reductions of the way of Christ in love (5:1–2), in Spirit-filling (5:18), and in wisdom (5:15–17). The instructions to wives, husbands, children, fathers, slaves, and masters are instances of what love, the Spirit-filled life, and wisdom look like in the household. But the places to begin, if we truly want to get a good grip on today's passage, are first not with our own contexts and traditions. I like what Lynn Cohick writes, "Maybe we start with what Paul said, rather than with our own presuppositions or questions. For example, in discussing husbands, Paul does not mention roles such as protector or provider. Paul does not speak of leadership or authority as part of the oneness of the marriage. What new images, pictures, metaphors, and stories, based on what Paul wants husbands to think about, can be substituted for our cultural expectations?" (Cohick, Proclamation, 110). Second, we need to begin with a serious sketch of the cultural world-view of the household at that time.

WORLDVIEW

To Aristotle's famous and massively influential book, *Politics*, we turn because it represents both the philosopher and the commoner, both what Paul had learned in the home and what he saw in other homes. Families are part of social order, beginning with the state, and they look like this:

107

For husbands and wives: "And since, as we saw, the science of household management has three divisions, one the relation of master to slave, of which we have spoken before, one the paternal relation, and the third the conjugal—for it is a part of the household science to rule over wife and children (over both as over freemen, yet not with the same mode of government, but over the wife to exercise republican government and over the children monarchical); for the male is by nature better fitted to command than the female (except in some cases where their union has been formed contrary to nature) . . . . (1.5.1–2)

For fathers and children: "The rule of the father over the children on the other hand is that of a king; for the male parent is the ruler in virtue both of affection and of seniority, which is characteristic of royal government." (1.5.2)

For masters and slaves: "Since therefore property is a part of a household and the art of acquiring property a part of household management (for without the necessaries even life, as well as the good life, is impossible), and since, just as for the particular arts it would be necessary for the proper tools to be forthcoming if their work is to be accomplished, so also the manager of a household must have his tools, and of tools some are lifeless and others living (for example, for a helmsman the rudder is a lifeless tool and the look-out man a live tool—for an assistant in the arts belongs to the class of tools), so also an article of property is a tool for the purpose of life, and property generally is a collection of tools, and a slave is a live article of property" (1.2.3–4).

If you paid attention to the references in Aristotle's famous book you will have noticed the numbers are in reverse order. Aristotle began at what he considered the bottom (he called it the "smallest parts") of the household. Turning to the Jewish world, we can dip into Josephus, a first century Jewish historian, who wrote this about women: "A woman is inferior to a man in all respects" . . . so "let her obey, not that she may be abused, but that she may be ruled" . . . "for God has given power to the man" (*Against Apion*, 201). Josephus, an aristocrat and priest, believed the purpose of sexual relations was procreation (199), that same-sex relations deserved the death penalty (199), and that abortion was to be prohibited (202).

These words best sum up how households in the world of Paul's letter were managed: power was assigned to the head of the household, nearly always a man, and thus the system was a patriarchy (which means rule by the father, or the father is first). A strict hierarchy or ordering became intuitive and institutional. This hierarchy reflected status and formed into a superior-inferior order. Put baldly, the ancient world thought women were inferior to men, and slaves were inferior to the free. We must start there to comprehend today's reading.

GENERAL OBSERVATIONS

People of color in the USA, women, rural Americans, people with disabilities, and anyone else who has been socially marginalized, experience what Paul writes as a *reinforcement* of unjust social orders. As we read today's passage, we need to keep in mind how these texts have been used against the non-dominant culture. The sketch of worldview above leads to a few general observations comparing Paul with the worldview at his time. My experience in teaching about the household regulations has been that the following observations are steps toward a radical paradigm shift, both for many today who were nurtured in a patriarchal, authoritarian, hierarchical worldview but also for first century Christians. So, each of these points substantively shifts how the household looked for Christians.

First, Paul chose to locate his instructions in households as they were anchored in his world. His Greek and Roman audiences would have expected this order, but they would have been stunned at times by what he had to say. Second, Paul *flips the order* of the people: instead of husband-wife, father-children, master-slave, we have wife-husband, children-father, slave-master. Paul begins, then, with the subordinate and then follows the superordinate. This is unusual, almost unprecedented, and evocative of changes he is making. Third, notice that the superordinate is assumed to have power, *but the instructions diminish the superordinate's power and authority, and thus they prohibit abuses of power.* Which leads, then, to fourth: since the power of the superordinate is diminished, the traditional subordinate is *empowered.* Each of the subordinates would have immediately sensed the winds of change. Thus, fifth, the subordinates in each case *are given agency to choose and to take responsibility* in how they related to the superordinate. Paul, sixth, expected the subordinates and superordinates to behave in a manner that was Christian.

A final observation reveals that what Paul is doing in the household regulations is Christianizing them. The motivations for behaviors are not shaped by the state and its powers (Athens, Rome, Ephesus) but by Christian ethics. Thus, for wives we see not *because your husband has authority* but "as to the Lord" (5:22; *Second Testament*). For children, we read not *because your father has authority* but "for this is right" (6:1). But when it comes to slaves, we get a radical change: "Obey them not only to win their favor when their eye is on you, but as slaves of Christ, doing the will of God from your heart. Serve wholeheartedly, as if you were serving the Lord, not people, because you know that the Lord will reward each one for whatever good they do, whether they are slave or free" (6:6–8). Masters, too, are given a Christian basis: "since you know that he who is both their Master and yours is in heaven, and there is no favoritism with him" (6:9). What is not mentioned here, but which is mentioned in 1 Peter 2:11–3:7, is that the intent of good behavior in the home may be that the early Christians acquire and sustain a good reputation for good citizens, rather than rebellious.

MUTUALITY

The particular instructions for the members of a household begin at verse twenty-two but they only get their start with an instruction *that applies to each of the household members* in verse twenty-one, which reads, "ordering yourselves under one another in awe of Christos" (*Second Testament*). And verse twenty-one's "ordering yourselves under" is a participle that modifies "Be filled with the Spirit," which is followed by the following participles:

> Be filled with the Spirit
> > By speaking . . .
> > By singing . . .
> > By making music . . .
> > By giving thanks . . .
> > By ordering yourselves under . . .

To make this more complex, "Be filled" joins other orders by Paul, which begin at least at verse fifteen: "Be very careful . . . do not be foolish . . . understand . . . do not get drunk . . .

be filled with the Spirit." As I said, it's a long section, and one could begin even before 5:15.

Now to 5:21 and 5:22. The wife's ordering under her husband continues with the same verb (ordering-under), though that action is implied and not explicitly stated for the wife. Thus, "Wives to your own husbands" is a literal translation. Because of the larger context, ordering-under manifests love, wisdom, and the Spirit-filled life. From a slightly different angle, these three important reductions constrain the meaning of "ordering yourselves under one another," which remember they are to be done with a singular motivation: "in awe of Christos." All the statuses mentioned—wives, husbands, children, fathers, slaves, masters—are to commit to ordering-under. This also means that the husband's love for his wife is an instance of "ordering yourselves under *one another*," which makes it mutual. The children's obedience is complemented by the father's "ordering yourselves under one another" in not intentionally irritating the children. The enslaved person's obedience is also matched by the master's connecting all of his (or her) powers to serving the Lord. There is then some irony in Paul's choice of terms: the "under" is subverted by the mutuality of the instructions! Our emphasis, then, is to be on ordering, which refers to social order (not commanding). Paul thus does not endorse the first century's cultural hierarchies; he inserts a Christian ethic into that order and so re-orders it! What are not characteristic of grace in the home are power and authority.

If mutual submission of verse twenty-one is taken seriously, it re-defines each of the behaviors for each of the statuses in the Christian household. The state disappears in Paul's household regulations, and in the place of the state we find the Lord Jesus Christ reshaping how family members are to live with one another. We can now turn to the specifics in light of these larger themes, and in so doing we

will encounter an early Christian attempt to let Christ rule
the home. The most important change that happens is that
the patriarchy, hierarchy, and unchecked power of the head
of the household have met the Lord. The word "submit" no
longer has the sense of power over but now means power
for the empowerment of the other. Many today have failed
the basic reading of this text in its context and have instead
concentrated attention and instruction on the *authority of the
man (husband, father, master)*. That approach replaces Paul
with Aristotle. Paul does not want the Christians to go back
to Aristotle. A new order is in view. This is why I have translated the Greek term *hypotassō* with "order under" instead
of "submit." I believe "order under" provides more breathing
space for agency and choice, while "submit" evokes power
and authority and a lack of agency.

WIVES AND HUSBANDS

Marriages flourish most when the woman and the man love
one another deeply, not when they live out the script of some
pre-conceived role for a woman and a man. There is a harm-
ful tendency to reduce husbands and wives to roles, to what
the American poet Christian Wiman describes as a "character pinched to characteristic" (Wiman, "To Eat the Awful,"
8). Roles reduce a person to a persona or a person into a
personality type. As if God designed women to be led and
men to lead. Nothing like that is said in this text, though
some have made it the central point of the passage. Rather,
Paul instructs wives, who here have agency and choice, to
order themselves under their husbands because their action
is done "as to the Lord." A comment on "submit to your husbands in everything" needs to be made. The larger context
baptizes both ordering-under and "in everything" into the
waters of Christian behaviors. A Christian wife does not

steal because her husband tells her to. "Paul is not saying that the husband's sexual, financial, recreational, familial or any other preferences take priority over his wife's preferences" (Cohick, Proclamation, 106; cf. 1 Corinthians 7:1–7). She instead chooses to order herself in relation to her husband in a way that comports with Christlikeness.

Paul labels the man—there is actually no Greek word for "husband" so the term is "man"—the "head," which is another term of controversy. Many suggest the term means authority over. Head is a metaphor; metaphors have to be interpreted; metaphors teach us to think of a husband the way we think of a head, and not everything about the latter pertains to the former. In 4:15–16 head was about the source of growth; in 1:21 it referred to rule. In both cases, the head is Christ.

In this context, we need to explore the metaphor. First, it is Christlikeness, and the Christlikeness explicitly mentioned is saving, not ruling. Second, the wife's relation to her husband parallels the church's relation to Jesus Christ, which entails a redemptive ordering under. Saving is not the same as being an authority. Third, a husband's ordering-under relation to his wife means "love" with a Christlike love (5:25), and that love is a saving love that, like all love, works toward growth in Christlikeness. Paul uses these terms for redemption-shaped Christlikeness: holy, cleansing, washing with water through the word, and presenting her to God as "holy and blameless" (5:26–27). Here, then, is a radical move by Paul. In Aristotle's world women could not be friends with their husbands because they could not attain that level of ethical maturity. They were inferior to men. Paul exhorts husbands to nurture Christlikeness in their wives by loving them in a Christlike manner, creating a culture of equity and equality (5:28). Thus, the husband is called to exemplify Christ in love. Paul, so it would seem, ought to have called the husband to submission/ordering under as he did the wife. I say this because both "ordering under" in 5:22 and "love" in 5:25 are specific instances of "ordering yourselves under one another in awe of Christ" in 5:21. But first century folks could not have comprehended a wife "ordering under" her husband, so Paul Christianizes ordering under with "love." Which, in my view, is indistinguishable from ordering under. Paul sees true love in the sacrifice of Christ for the sake of the world. Love is sacrifice for the other. As Lynn Cohick explains, wives were legally "minors" in that world (Cohick, *Ephesians*, 352). Paul goes as far as he can perceive.

Paul, in his customary way, finds himself in a sidebar reflection. Christ unites himself to humans in the body of Christ, and husbands and wives are united to one another just as Genesis says (Genesis 2:24). The two become one, and their oneness exemplifies the secret union of Christ and the church. So, Paul sums up the husband's relationship to his wife as loving her as much as he loves himself, and the wife then can "awe" her husband's loving, wise, Spirit-filled acts of mutual ordering of one another (Ephesians 5:21). At no point does Paul say a husband has authority over a wife; at no point does he say the husband leads his wife. Four different times in this short passage Paul tells the husband to *love* his wife. His mutual submission, then, is love, with love understood as sacrifice for the other. A wife's submission is her recipro-cal love in the mutual act of wise and Spirit-shaped love of one another. As an aside, when marriage turns into language about authority and who is in charge, the marriage is on the rocks. Marriages need love to flourish.

CHILDREN AND FATHERS

Addressing children in this context names them, identi-fies them, dignifies them, and gives them a place in the community. A child's responsibility in mutual ordering under is to "obey" one's parents but they do so with agency: "in the Lord." Which makes it "right" (6:1). Paul anchors this in the first of the ten commandments by quoting Deuteronomy 5:16. The mutuality part for the father, and he switches here from "parents" (6:1) to "fathers" (6:4), means not intentionally irritating or exasperating their children. Here, Paul presents a mutuality, an interactive relationship between children and fathers, and there is agency for the child in this relationship.

Involved in this interactive relationship is that fathers are responsible (in that world this was primarily the father's responsibility, but not always done by himself) to "nurture them in Lord's education and mentoring" (6:4, *Second Testament*). Mothers were often involved in the education of children, too. Remember that Timothy learned scriptures from his mother and grandmother (2 Timothy 1:5). Education in the first century was overwhelmingly emulation instead of information. Paul has in mind a father exemplifying what it means to live "in the Lord," and in the context of this letter, it meant exemplifying love, wisdom, Spirit-filled living, and the interactive relationship where each person learns about and nurtures the other. One of my favorite Substacks is by Shane Wood, called "Letters from the Desert." Recently he talked about how some academics fear AI (artificial intelligence). Shane's response takes us straight back to first century education:

> The problem isn't A.I., though, but an artificial definition of education. One passed on from generation to generation by student and professor alike. Education, so the story goes, is a system of transmitting knowledge for payment, disclosing secrets of a trade for remuneration. The problem, then, is quite clear: Artificial

Intelligence accomplishes this more efficiently, expansively, and economically.

Insert fear.

But what if education was more than merely buying and selling information? What if it was a journey? Wholistic? Targeting the heart, soul, mind, and strength of the student? What if education was something more akin to a testimony; an exploration; a mutual pursuit of truth inhabited and enfleshed, not just memorized and parroted?

Paul's understanding of education for parents was about mentoring, being with, guiding, interacting, engaging with disagreements, and caring for the formation of a child into Christlikeness. Authority and power are not in mind.

ENSLAVED PERSONS AND SLAVEOWNERS

Noticeably there are more words about the enslaved than the masters (masters were slaveowners), so let's call them what they were. In this context, we can't delve into enslavement in the ancient world (here I will reproduce what I wrote in *1&2 Timothy, Titus, Philemon*, 80–81). The most important words Paul uses here are "slavery" and "slave." Keith Bradley, one of the world's experts on Roman slavery, defines it as it should be defined: "Slavery by definition is a means of securing and maintaining an involuntary labour force by a group in society which monopolises political and economic power" (Bradley, *Slaves and Masters*, 18).

Slavery in the Roman world was about status and integrity and identity, all three reshaped by turning a person into a utility. Most slaves were born into slavery, and a slave's life was dependent upon the master's character. A male slave remained in the status of a "boy" his entire life, unless emancipated, in order to prevent a legal marriage, legal control of (their non-legal marital relationship) children, and thus legal inheritance rights. Slaves were commonly abused physically and sexually, and many female slaves were sex slaves to their masters. I want to make two observations, and they will not be comfortable for some. First it is a very, very serious mistake to pretend that slavery then was not the same as slavery in the New World. It's a similar mistake to think of Roman slavery along the lines of modern employment. A slave is an owned body. Furthermore, the word "slave" is a label that devalues a person's dignity, agency, and social status. It is better to say, "enslaved person" than "slave." Second, Paul and his co-workers did not perceive the immorality and hideousness of slavery. They swam in waters boiling with slavery and did not perceive they were boiling themselves. There is nothing about this slavery text that transfers into our world easily. Yes, it was beneficial for those who lived in a world of slavery to work in a way that did not get the gospel mission into any more trouble than it already was. Yes, it is good for people to work for their bosses as people who are serving God and not their bosses, but this text is not about pragmatism, workers, and bosses, but about masters and slaves. It belongs in that world, and I shall leave it there. Paul's teaching here, and elsewhere, has been abused by slaveowners and used to justify violence, rape, and exploitation. American history was (mis)shaped by these verses, and systemic racism names it.

What Paul advises in wisdom and with an insufficient amount of Spirit-filling was for the enslaved person—who is named and seen by Paul—to use her or his agency by ordering themselves under the slaveowner, and to do so in a way that exemplified the way of Jesus. Their relationship is not one of inferior-superior, but of siblings in Christ. He ties the enslaved to the slaveowner the way he ties the church to Christ, and thus in the way he ties women to their husbands (6:5; cf. to 5:25). Paul enhances and emboldens their agency when he instructs them not to work to gain the favor of their slaveowner but to work as "slaves of Christ," which means "doing the will of God from your heart" and doing so seeking the approval, not of men, but only of God (6:6–8). This is a powerful diminishment, at some level resistant if not potentially rebellious, of the slaveowner's privileged power and authority.

Paul instructs the slaveowners in fewer words, but once again there is not a shred of evidence that he wants them to act with authority. No, he diminishes their power by saying they, too, are to relate to their enslaved persons as one who answers to God—not to Rome, not to Ephesus, not to Athens, and not to social norms. Paul's words are brief but what he says is this: "do the same things to" the enslaved as they are doing to the slaveowners (*Second Testament*). That is, relate to one another in a manner shaped by the gospel, not by the social standards of the day. Esau McCaulley thinks these words are "paradigm-shifting" (McCaulley, "Ephesians," 435). God is the judge of both the enslaved and the slaveowners (6:9), and that means they will each be judged according to how Christian their treatment of each other was. It is not hard to see when the love of God and love of Christ and love of self shape the enslaved person's relationship. Love of God, Christ, and self is also to shape the slaveowner's treatment of the enslaved. But I would contend that the person who is truly Spirit-filled will perceive the immorality of slavery. The vast majority of Christians for the first twenty centuries of the church did not perceive this, and many don't today.

We do. We have agency. It is ours to do what is right. Today.

QUESTIONS FOR REFLECTION
AND APPLICATION

1. Take a moment to imagine a household in Ephesus: householder, family members, extended family, slaves, tenants. How do you think each of them would feel when hearing Paul's words in this section read aloud in their house church assembly?

2. How do the writings from Aristotle and Josephus illustrate a superior-inferior ordering of household relationships?

3. What are some of the rhetorical techniques Paul uses when writing about household ordering to flip the paradigm his audience would have been expecting?

4. What do you see as the differences between living out "submit" versus living out "order under"?

5. What would you like to shift in your relationships as you seek to "order yourself under" your siblings in Christ—your family members or those with whom you are close?

FOR FURTHER READING

Aristotle, *Politics*, Loeb Classical Library (Cambridge, Massachusetts: Harvard University Press, 1998) (trans. H. Rackham).

Keith R. Bradley, *Slaves and Masters in the Roman Empire: A Study in Social Control* (New York: Oxford University Press, 1987).

Josephus, *Against Apion: Translation and Commentary*, by John M.G. Barclay (Leiden: Brill, 2013).

Scot McKnight, *1&2 Timothy, Titus, Philemon*, Everyday Bible Study: New Testament (Grand Rapids: HarperChristian Resources, 2023), 207–208. For more, see my *The Letter to Philemon*, New International Commentary on the New Testament (Grand Rapids: Wm. B. Eerdmans, 2017), 1–36.

Christian Wiman, "To Eat the Awful While You Starve Your Awe," in *Survival is a Style* (New York: Farrar, Straus and Giroux, 2020).

Shane Wood, "I Disagree." https://shanejwood.substack.com/p/i-disagree.

GRACE IN ARMOR

Ephesians 6:10–24

[10] *Finally, be strong in the Lord and in his mighty power.* [11] *Put on the full armor of God, so that you can take your stand against the devil's schemes.* [12] *For our struggle is not against flesh and blood, but against the rulers, against the authorities, against the powers of this dark world and against the spiritual forces of evil in the heavenly realms.* [13] *Therefore put on the full armor of God, so that when the day of evil comes, you may be able to stand your ground, and after you have done everything, to stand.* [14] *Stand firm then, with the belt of truth buckled around your waist, with the breastplate of righteousness in place,* [15] *and with your feet fitted with the readiness that comes from the gospel of peace.* [16] *In addition to all this, take up the shield of faith, with which you can extinguish all the flaming arrows of the evil one.* [17] *Take the helmet of salvation and the sword of the Spirit, which is the word of God.*

[18] *And pray in the Spirit on all occasions with all kinds of prayers and requests. With this in mind, be alert and always keep on praying for all the Lord's people.* [19] *Pray also for me, that whenever I speak, words may be given me so that I will fearlessly make known the mystery of the gospel,* [20] *for which I am an ambassador in chains. Pray that I may declare it fearlessly, as I should.*

[21] *Tychicus, the dear brother and faithful servant in the Lord,*

will tell you everything, so that you also may know how I am and what I am doing. [22] *I am sending him to you for this very purpose, that you may know how we are, and that he may encourage you.*

[23] *Peace to the brothers and sisters, and love with faith from God the Father and the Lord Jesus Christ.* [24] *Grace to all who love our Lord Jesus Christ with an undying love.*

Had Paul lived in our day and combined core biblical virtues with features of America's military industry and machine, we might experience what the first century Christians experienced, and we might also cringe. Here is a paraphrastic translation of 6:10–17 doing just that.

> Be empowered in God and in the grip of God's strength. Suit up in God's gear so you will have the commanding authority to resist the enemy's strategies. We are not wrestling with this nation or that army, but with cosmic rulers, with authorities in digital camo, with global defense systems of darkness, with the axis of evil disguised in empires.
>
> So be a geardo* for God's gear so, when the war starts, you will have the power to resist on that day of evil and, having battled to the end, you will be left standing over the enemy. Establish your force's borders, outfitted with:
>
> > Truth's tactical belt,
> > Suited up with justice's bulletproof vest,
> > Strapping on preparation with the peace-gospel's boots,
>
> In all this, be a geardo with the shield of allegiance (with which you can ward off the enemy's high-powered

---

* Military lingo for one obsessed with military outfits and gear.

ammo). And be a geardo with freedom's ballistic helmet and the Spirit's weapon, which is God's utterance.

This paraphrase attempts to use modern military terms that function in similar ways to the terms Paul chose. Let's talk about his choice of terms.

Since we are not first-century Ephesians who were overly familiar with the outfits and weapons of war in Rome-based armies, and even more since we have become so familiar with Paul's use of military gear for the Christian "geardo," we fail to see how jarring of an image military outfits can be for depicting the Christian life. Military gear and the militia are put into play for only two reasons: protecting a people from war and going to war to defeat an enemy. Paul has chosen to end this letter with images that construct the Christian life as a war against an enemy. He has chosen to end with metaphors, and metaphors teach us to think of one thing (Christian life) in terms of another thing (military outfit). Yet, we may cringe that these images depict humans dealing death to other humans in wars over resources and locations driven by undeniable ego-drenched contests of narcissists. I confess that using military images for the Christian life might legitimate violence for some. As cartoons, video gaming, apocalyptic (Marvel) movies, and TV shows in which violence looms large have an impact on people to become violent, so Paul's imagery here can predispose some to violence. We need to be aware of this as we read it, as it impacts us, and as we teach or pass it on. I utter an Amen to Will Willimon who in a sermon said, "I have trouble with military metaphors as descriptions of the Christian life" (Willimon, *Collected Sermons*, 76). Marilynne Robinson once wrote words I underlined and have returned to with benefit often: "No war will end, short of Armageddon. So we had better consider other options" (Robinson, *What Are We Doing*

Here?, 116–117). Paul offers to us today one of those other options, and in his offer, he transforms military gear into spiritual battle.

Having issued a detailed warning, I want to endorse the moral virtues at work in Paul's imagery and to remind us that Paul's language echoes terms from Isaiah (esp. 59:17; see also 11:4–5; 52:7). His terms are: God's empowering powers in us, resisting the evil one and its minions at work in our world's systems, truth, righteousness/justice, the gospel of peace, faith/allegiance, liberation/salvation, and the Spirit's work in the Word of God. We can become geardos in the redemptive work of God in this world without using violence and without going all macho. But most of us might choose to focus on the virtues and drop the military gear. Lynn Cohick warns us against any suggestions of triumphalism because the battle is, after all, cosmic and not with armies and battalions (Cohick, *Proclamation*, 134).

THE BATTLE IS COSMIC

I mentioned Willimon's worry about military language above, but when he has asked what people think of when they sing the war-drenched hymn "The Battle Hymn of the Republic," they answered, "The civil rights movement." He adds this important word: "Perhaps we forget, in a time of tame churches, toned-down preachers, and timid prophets that there was a time when the church believed that there was something worth fighting for" (Willimon, *Collected Sermons*, 77). I take his words as a warning to me, too. We can, in this need to go to battle, learn a big lesson from our minority friends. They grow up without social power, knowing the system doesn't work as advertised, experiencing questions about their race or their ethnicity, who can rise in the system with the system's help, only to discover that those who are white are the most preferred in jobs, whose systems are normative, whose leaders are the most respected, who have access to the most resources, and who are free to be who they are—all the while their white privileges, called "systemic whiteness," is, like the emperor's "new clothes," invisible to themselves but all the minorities see right through it all day long every day for their entire lives (summarizing themes in Edwards and Kim, *Estranged Pioneers*, 116–149).

Minority cultures, I am saying, experience a cosmic system against them or at least resisting their attempts to succeed. The powers that prevent their success are invisible and more than they can defeat. Transfer this now to Paul's language about the cosmic battle, and we have a near-perfect analogy. The powers emerge from the "evil trickster" (6:11; *First Nations*). The "devil's schemes" are not reducible to what we see in "flesh and blood" but are at work in the rulers and authorities and this world's dark powers that embed the "spiritual forces of evil" (6:10–12).

CHRISTIAN VIRTUES FOR THE BATTLE

The virtues mentioned in our passage are found elsewhere in Ephesians (1:13, 15; 4:24; 2:14–18). So, we turn to each now. The belt he has in mind was worn around the waist but had several wide straps hanging down from it, skirt-like, to protect from the belly down to the knees. The cloak was tucked into it to give legs freedom to move. We are to buckle up with *truth*, a term that is used for Jesus himself (John 14:6), the revelation of God's will and ways (Romans 2:8), the gospel (15:8; Galatians 2:5, 14; 5:7; Ephesians 1:13; 4:21), and quite often to the moral practice of transparency in what one says and claims (2 Corinthians 4:2; 6:7; 7:14; 12:6; Ephesians 4:25; 5:9). In today's reading the term truth refers to the gospel message and the fearless standing for it and speaking about it (6:14). In the battle against systemic evil speaking the truth over time unravels the evil system. (Over time, I must emphasize.)

When Paul uses the term *righteousness*, symbolized here in the breastplate which was often used to display one's achievements and status, his entire understanding of the Bible comes into play: the term describes the relationship of consistency between a standard and practices. God is the standard, and God reveals the standard in the law of Moses and in the ethics of Jesus as lived in the Holy Spirit. A Spirit-filled person practices righteousness. As such, the term "justice" and "righteousness" overlap significantly. The apostle Paul adapted the behavioral understanding of the term (doing what is right; Matthew 5:20) so that it referred to one's declared status in Christ (Romans 5:1; 10:3–4; 2 Corinthians 5:21), a status that leads to transformation into a person who behaves righteously (6:13, 16–20; 8:10; 9:30–31; 14:17; Ephesians 4:24). A life marked by God's redemptive work of righteousness in us that transforms us into agents of doing what is right in this world counters the systemic evils of our day. For example, Mr. Rogers was good for the world because he was a man who did what was right and sought to be a good neighbor to all.

The *gospel of peace* that Paul speaks about here is a gospel that defeats evil and brings light into the darkness, both interpersonally but especially in our spheres of influence. The gospel brings peace. I quote what I have written elsewhere:

> A sketch of the meaning of the term peace in the New Testament reveals that God is a God of peace, the message is a gospel of peace, the gospel makes peace with God, and thus believers are to pursue peace among themselves and with others. Paul greets his churches with peace and

Paul reminds the Corinthians—with whom he had at least a strained relationship—that the Christian calling is to live in peace. One of the most important visions of the early Christians is found in Ephesians 2, when Paul says Christ is himself the peace that unites gentiles with Jews. That theme expands to cosmic peace in another letter of Paul's, the one to the Colossians.

Peace needs to be pressed into action because war and peace cannot themselves be the simultaneous callings of those who follow the way of Jesus. One can't mitigate peace with war and contend for following the teachings of the New Testament.*

Paul's penchant is that grace is unleashed by shield-like *faith*, and by faith Paul means the act of trusting God, of trusting God to redeem us in Christ, the ongoing act of trust as allegiance to Christ, and the substance of what we believe as The Faith. If we are to stand against the cosmic systems of evil at work in our world, we will need to stand for truth, to stand for doing what is right at the right time, to stand for peace when enmity and war are on the horizon, and to live a life of allegiance to Christ as the world's true Lord. Each of these are sharp instruments of defeat against the ways of the evil one and evil.

The impact of these virtues derives from the gospel that redeems us in Christ. Paul uses a term that was as common in the public statements of Rome as it was in the pages of his Bible. We often translate it as *salvation*, but the term draws us into the world of liberation and release from captivity

---

* I appealed to Romans 16:20; Acts 10:36; Ephesians 6:15; Romans 5:1; 14:19; Galatians 1:3; 1 Corinthians 7:15; Ephesians 2:14–18; Colossians 1:19–20, in the footnote to this lengthy quotation from my book *The Bible is Not Enough: Imagination and Making Peace in the Modern World* (Minneapolis: Fortress, 2023), 6.

and deliverance and rescue—and what humans are liberated (etc.) from is holistic: spiritual, social, physical, emotional, psychological, relational, and systemic. Spirit-filled, loving, wise Christians are outfitted through the Spirit to be agents of liberation in this world.

Finally, Paul takes us in a fresh way right back to Ephesians 5:18's words about the Spirit-filled life by urging believers to take hold of the "sword of the Spirit," which he then defines as *God's utterance*, or words we hear and speak that derive from the Spirit of God (6:17). Everything Paul says from 4:17 through today's reading is about a life filled with the Spirit.

GETTING PERSONAL

Paul resumes, so I think, that string of participles we encountered way back in 5:18–21 (speaking, singing, playing the strings, thanking, and ordering-under) when in 6:18 he suddenly uses a participle again. The NIV makes it an imperative (as it did to a participle in 5:21) with "And pray in the Spirit" (6:18), but I prefer "Praying in the Spirit" (*Second Testament*). He wants them to pray for all things and at all times, including prayers for himself so that he can boldly declare the truth of the gospel—that is, that he will be outfitted for the task given to him by God—despite that he is in prison for his mission work's message (6:19–20). His close co-worker Tychicus has all the goods about Paul they may need to know, and he says the same to the Christians of Colossae (6:21–22; cf. Colossians 4:7).

Paul taps on the Shut Down or the Sleep key with a blessing of *peace* and *love* that he mediates to them from God, the Father of the Lord Jesus Christ, and—no surprise here—*grace*, the power of God behind it all, a power that will never decay or erode (6:23–24).

QUESTIONS FOR REFLECTION
AND APPLICATION

1. What is your visceral reaction to reading the modern military paraphrase of these verses? How does it feel to reflect on this imagery?

2. How does racism function as one illustration of a "cosmic system" that needs to be battled against?

3. Which element of this armored preparation do you most need in your life: truth, righteousness, the gospel of peace, faith, salvation/liberation, God's utterance?

4. As a Christian today, where do you need to go to battle?

5. What is your most important takeaway from this study of Ephesians?

FOR FURTHER READING

Korie Little Edwards, Rebecca Y. Kim, *Estranged Pioneers: Race, Faith, and Leadership in a Diverse World* (New York: Oxford, 2024).

Scot McKnight, *The Bible is Not Enough: Imagination and Making Peace in the Modern World* (Minneapolis: Fortress, 2023).

Marilynne Robinson, *What Are We Doing Here? Essays* (New York: Farrar, Staus and Giroux, 2018).

William H. Willimon, *The Collected Sermons of William H. Willimon* (Louisville: Westminster John Knox, 2010).

COLOSSIANS

GROWING IN VIRTUE

Colossians 1:1–14

¹ Paul, an apostle of Christ Jesus by the will of God, and Timothy our brother,

² To God's holy people in Colossae, the faithful brothers and sisters in Christ:

Grace and peace to you from God our Father.

³ We always thank God, the Father of our Lord Jesus Christ, when we pray for you, ⁴ because we have heard of your faith in Christ Jesus and of the love you have for all God's people—⁵ the faith and love that spring from the hope stored up for you in heaven and about which you have already heard in the true message of the gospel ⁶ that has come to you. In the same way, the gospel is bearing fruit and growing throughout the whole world—just as it has been doing among you since the day you heard it and truly understood God's grace. ⁷ You learned it from Epaphras, our dear fellow servant, who is a faithful minister of Christ on our behalf, ⁸ and who also told us of your love in the Spirit.

⁹ For this reason, since the day we heard about you, we have not stopped praying for you. We continually ask God to fill you with the knowledge of his will through all the wisdom and understanding that the Spirit gives, ¹⁰ so that you may live a life worthy of the Lord and please him in every way: bearing fruit in every good work, growing in the knowledge of God, [11] being strengthened with all power according to his glorious might so that you may have great endurance and patience, [12] and giving joyful thanks to the Father, who has qualified you to share in the inheritance of his holy people in the kingdom of light. [13] For he has rescued us from the dominion of darkness and brought us into the kingdom of the Son he loves, [14] in whom we have redemption, the forgiveness of sins.

Publishers today credit the author or authors of a book by putting their name on the cover. On my shelf, I'm looking at a book called *Jesus Among the Gods* by my friend Michael F. Bird, whose name is put on the spine and on the title page. Near that book is one entitled *New Testament Theology*, by G.B. Caird, and just below his name on the title page we read "Completed and edited by L.D. Hurst." On the spine we read "Caird and Hurst." On another shelf I have a book, *Voices Long Silenced*, by Joy A. Schroeder and Marion Ann Taylor. One written by one author; one completed by another author; and one co-written by two authors. Credit is given where credit is due.

In the church, Paul has been given all the credit for Colossians, but he does not claim the credit for all of it. Paul puts a solid *and* before Timothy's name (see Acts 16:1–5; Philippians 2:19–24). Most of us ignore the *and* to think of this letter to the Colossians as *Paul's* letter. Very few occasionally write "Paul *and* Timothy" when referring to the authors. Expect changes in what follows! Margaret MacDonald, in her excellent commentary, clarifies how Paul wrote letters: "Paul's ministry is a collaborative effort involving a network of relationships," letter writing included (MacDonald, *Colossians*, 31). The two of them collaborated so equally in the production of this letter they topped it off with "Paul and Timothy."

In today's passage, which looks very much like the openings in Paul's other letters, solo author or co-author, we get a sampling of the present virtues of the Colossians, about whom he has heard from their co-worker Epaphras (1:7; *Second Testament:* "our loved co-slave"), but then they turn to a summary of their prayer and petitions for them to grow into other virtues. A note on Epaphras: Dennis Edwards writes about Paul speaking of Epaphras as a "co-slave." He writes, "on the one hand, African Americans might view Paul's appropriation of slave to describe his own ministry as insensitive, or even offensive. . . . On the other hand, Paul might be honoring enslaved people by pointing to them as models of devotion. . . . Perhaps rather than pity our fore-bears, we can see them instead as heroes; they persevered through hellish opposition" (D. Edwards, "Colossians," 484).

Our prayers for others tend to be very particular but, when compared with Paul's more abstract prayer requests, ours tend to be thin, even half-hearted and superficial at times. I doubt either Paul or Timothy prayed "God bless the missionaries and the mission churches"! We are about to discover what Paul asked for in praying for the Colossians and others, which leads to this observation. Not only do we tend to credit only Paul for this letter, but we forget Paul wanted this letter passed on to Laodicea (and probably Hierapolis; 4:13–16). Two authors writing up a letter for three churches—that's what we are about to dip into.

PRESENT VIRTUES

Paul was a man who praised others. In this letter, Paul describes himself as a "Commissioner . . . through God's plan," but the terms he uses for others ought to grab our attention. Timothy is "the brother" (1:1; *Second Testament;* the NIV draws Timothy closer to Paul by adding "our"). The Colossians are "the devoted and allegiant siblings in

Christos" (1:2; *Second Testament*; on "in Christ," see pp. 3 on Eph 1:1–10 above). The word *devoted* is *holy* in the NIV, which is the traditional translation of *hagios*. That term for Jewish authors like Paul and Timothy sits in a complex of no less than four ideas:

1. God alone is holy,
2. all things in God's presence must be holy,
3. any human being or thing that enters into God's presence must be "devoted" to God by being properly prepared, and
4. what is devoted to God is separated from the world or the common order.

So, the term suggests the Colossians are separated from the world of Colossae and Asia Minor and Rome, but in the chain of ideas, separation is the last, not the first, idea at work in the term we often translate with "holy." It is short-sighted to say "holy" means "separated." It means devoted to the God who is holy or, better yet, the holy God has made someone fit for God's presence. The Colossians have been devoted to God because they are "in Christ" (1:2).

Call and Response

There is a call and response aspect of this pastoral expression of gratitude. The call and response in African American Christianity describes the back-and-forth communication between leader (typically the preacher, or musical soloist) and the congregation (or choir), as each respond to what they've heard from the other. Hearing (Col 1:4, 5, 6), along with learning (Col 1:7), and making known (Col 1:8) reflect the pattern of communication between the leaders Epaphras and Paul with the Colossians. Epaphras taught the gospel (Col 1:7) so that the Colossians heard the word of truth (Col 1:5–6). The gospel bore fruit in the lives of the Colossians (Col 1:6), so in turn, Paul heard of their faith (Col 1:4), their hope (Col 1:5), and their love (Col 1:4,8). Faith in Jesus and the community's faithfulness were communicated back and forth between the leaders and the congregation.

D. Edwards, "Colossians," 484.

They are not only holy/devoted, but they are *faithful*, a term that means they are *allegiant* to Christ as their Lord. In Christianity, this term refers far too often to a one-and-done decision of faith, or believing, and not often enough to ongoing faith and trust, and hence in *The Second Testament* for this verse I use the word "allegiant" (Bates, *Gospel Allegiance*). So, to break this down: the summons of Christ is for us to trust him, or to believe in him, or to have faith in him. The Greek word for faith (noun) is *pistis*, while the word for believe (verb) is *pisteuō*. It is unfortunate that the connection between the two is missed when we use faith for the noun and believe for the verb. Trust in Christ not only begins with a decision to trust but true faith or trust becomes ongoing trust, that is, allegiance to Jesus Christ to whom we have entrusted ourselves and our lives. Which is why Paul and Timothy ("we" at 1:3!) pray for them (1:4).

They know, too, of their *love* (1:4, 8). Love is a rugged, affective commitment to a person, to be with that person (presence), to be for that person (advocate), and to be in a relationship of mutual growth (direction) in the virtues mentioned in today's reading (or, Christlikeness). The Colossians are reported to be people who love "all God's people" (1:4). The Colossians then love those in Hierapolis and the Laodiceans and the Ephesians and the Thessalonians and the Philippians and the Corinthians and the Romans. If they got to one of these communities, they found fellowship with other siblings in Christ. They had learned to do good to all, but especially to fellow believers (Galatians 6:10).

The faith and love of the Colossians had formed out of their *hope* (1:5), which completes the famous early Christian triad of faith, hope, and love. This hope flowed directly out of the gospel they heard and to which they had turned over their lives. The gospel is a message about Jesus himself, and that Jesus of that gospel is Savior, Lord, and Messiah/King/Emperor. The hope is for the kingdom, for the whole cosmic order being made right by God, for justice and peace and love to rule the world. This hope, Paul and Timothy write, is "stored up for you in heaven," which ought not to be reduced to going up to heaven when we die (Wright, *Surprised*). It refers to the location where God's Throne Room is, where the Control Room is, and where the great plans of God are stored in secret and awaiting final and full revelation when heaven comes to earth. John calls this the New Heavens and the New Earth, and his spatial imagery is not "up there" but "down here" (Revelation 20–22). That hope generated the Colossians' faith and love.

Each member of this triad results from the gospel about Jesus Christ (1:5), and this gospel—Paul wants them to know just in case they didn't know it—is flourishing in the Roman empire. Many think Paul and Timothy wrote this letter from Rome, so it is in Rome that they hear from visitors (Acts 28:30–31) about the gospel's growth from Jerusalem through Asia Minor into Greece and on to what we today call

Italy. Or, which is just as likely, perhaps the letter was written from some prison in Ephesus (discussion in McKnight, *Colossians*, 34–39). One person from whom they are getting reports is Epaphras (Colossians 1:8). At the end of this letter, they tell us how Epaphras is pastorally laboring for those in Hierapolis and Laodicea (4:12–13).

So, when Paul and Timothy think of the Colossians, which they do all the time when they pray, they think of their faith, hope, and love. On these they want to develop virtues in which they can grow. In interceding, or praying, for the Colossians, these two early Christian greats were not just asking for blessings. No, to intercede is to stand with. Paul and Timothy brought the Colossians into the Throne Room, stood in front of them representing them, and interceded for them with God, just as Abraham (Genesis 18) and Moses (Numbers 21:7) did for others.

VIRTUES IN THEOLOGY

Paul's and Timothy's intercessions and petitions for the Colossians are both for knowledge and for living like a follower of Jesus or, to use other terms, for theological and ethical flourishing. The former arises because of the theological problems at work in Colossae (see 2:4, 8, 16–23) as well as the need to become even more faithful (2:6–7; 2:20–3:17, 3:18–4:1). David Pao points us in the right direction with these words: "while Paul is not intentionally providing us with a systematic teaching on how to pray properly, this prayer report nonetheless becomes a powerful model of prayer" (Pao, *Colossians*, 78).

Theology matters. Bad ideas, once they become fixed in a culture, distort not only truth but all the ideas connected to corrupted truths. Chapter two will bring the toxic ideas challenging the Colossians into play (2:8–23). In a recent book, Karl Vaters decries the toxic results deriving from too many American churches becoming entangled in thinking the bigger the church the better, which all comes from measuring a church by its numbers (Vaters, *De-sizing the Church*). Pastors became entrepreneurs where methods and metrics led to measuring success by how many butts were in the pews, bills in the plate, baptisms in the pool, and buildings on the campus. Credibility, and spiritual maturity, too, somehow got measured by the size of a church's crowd, the width of the stage, the size of the screens, and the number of buildings. Enough said. The bad idea was that numbers tell the story, and the results were that pastors were no longer spiritual mentors, and the Christian life was measured by being a member of the biggest church. In Colossae the bad ideas were about Christ, and those ideas distorted everything. But good ideas don't abolish toxicity. Good ideas can be corrupted by corrupted characters using good ideas, or by bad behaviors by people who "believe" in good ideas. Just because someone claims to believe that God loves all doesn't automatically turn such believers into people who also love all people.

So, Paul and Timothy ("we" in 1:9) pray to God to give them "knowledge" (or "perception"; *Second Testament*), and "wisdom" and "understanding" so they can be "growing in the knowledge of God" (1:9–10). They need theological perception from God, through the Spirit (1:9). What matters most is not just the acquisition of information but growth in wisdom, which is learning to live in God's world in God's way, which is revealed in Christ. Perceptive knowledge and understanding, which here are Spirit-prompted, morph into wisdom when the persons involved have formed good character. Wisdom is telling a distant spouse that, by committing to more time with the family, the spouse will dial down the number of hours working. Knowledge of the problem can lead to wisdom. Wisdom is listening to the Spirit communicate to a person that they are over the top in their anger, and that it's time for some inner cultivation. And the person turns toward inner formation. Wisdom then works on both sides: the person speaking and the person to whom the other speaks. Paul and Timothy pray the Colossians will listen to the Spirit (and to them), and that they will listen, learn, and grow in theological virtues.

VIRTUES IN BEHAVIORS

It's said often, and it ought to be. The goal of theology is not knowledge acquisition or even information gathering, but what many today call lived theology. Notice that Paul and Timothy use "so that" twice: "so that you may live a life worthy . . ." and "so that you may have great endurance" (1:10, 11). Good ideas, embraced in wisdom, form into good characters who practice good virtues, that is, they walk around doing what is good, which at times contrasts with the way others in Colossae walk around (cf. 1:10; 2:6; 3:7; 4:5).

One of these virtues is to live a life "worthy of the Lord and [to] please him in every way" (1:10). These authors want the Colossians to re-orient their hearts and minds away from what works in the forum of Colossae to what God wants. They want them to ask, whether they wear the bracelet or not, What Would God Think (WWGT). We all have imbibed from our primary socialization as infants and children the facial expressions of our parents, and as we grow, we learn to check our behaviors by what those we love reveal in their faces and words. Paul and Timothy long for the Colossians to turn their gaze from human faces to God's face, and they do this by learning from scriptures, the Spirit, and others what a life before God looks like. That life looks like Jesus. God does not impose his facial expressions on us like a tyrant or a perfectionist or an emotionless independent judge and jury. No, God loves us, and God's face is the face of love, of trust, of hope, of compassion, of understanding, and of wisdom. The *First Nations Version* admiringly takes us to the face of God with "making his heart glad," and since we cannot see the heart, we perceive a glad heart in the face (1:10). A worthy life breaks down into four participles, with the first two tied together more closely:

> bearing fruit and growing,
> being empowered,
> and giving thanks with joy (1:10, 11, 12).

The four participles also point to four features of spiritual formation. Spiritual growth, which opens up what a worthy life looks like, pervades this whole letter (as we will see).

A lived theology expresses itself in "bearing fruit in every good work" (1:10), which means the Colossians had learned and would continue to learn that they are called to be good people doing good works in the public sector, like providing grain during a famine, sponsoring a public event, caring for the poor, constructing a bridge, financing a teacher or traveling philosopher—not to gain attention and glory and honor, and not to manipulate their way into the heart of an unsuspecting unbeliever. Rather, they are to do good works because those works are good, and good people live a theology that transcends knowledge into a life that witnesses to the goodness of God in Christ.

All these virtues of behavior, we need to remind ourselves over and over, find their true source, not in our efforts, but in God: "in all power empowering in a manner consistent with his splendorous grip" so that the Colossians will "have great endurance and patience" (1:11). Our authors triple up on the importance of God as the source: power, empowering, and grip are words attached to what God in the Spirit does in and for us. A life that finds God's affirming face and good works that flourish into glory for God is a life empowered by the Spirit, not by our calculations, preparations, manipulations, educations, and excitations.

With all this in mind, Paul and Timothy turn from what can be seen as a moral life that exudes human agency, if not disciplined willpower, to a life that turns throughout a day to joyful thanksgiving to God for what God has done for us in Christ and for us in the Spirit (1:12–14). They construct here a lengthy sentence that strings us the listeners on from one theme to another. God has "made us adequate" for an "inheritance in the light" (*Second Testament*; NIV: "qualified us"; 1:12). "The Father has led believers into a new domain; their citizenship is now in a new kingdom" (MacDonald, *Colossians*, 51). That realm of light is then defined as "his loved Son's Empire."* As Dennis Edwards writes, "The government of Jesus is superior to any human government" (D. Edwards, "Colossians," 485). The authors expand on what these words mean. God rescues us, with an exodus-like salvation, from cosmic, systemic darkness and removes us into the Son's realm and rule (1:13). Their language evokes the exodus and entry into the land. His theme is then turned over into two more metaphors that this rescue and removal operation are all about: "liberation, release from sins" (1:14; *Second Testament*). Again, none of this happens because of us or them. God does this. The chain of thoughts and terms here come through best when we don't pause but let each one form next to the previous one.

Thanksgivings are truly in order, and we can ask for the prayer of Stanley Hauerwas to be ours:

---

* The NIV adds "the *kingdom* of the light" but the Greek text does not have "kingdom" there; it is with the Son's Empire (or kingdom). So, the NIV doubles the use of "kingdom" (1:12, 13).

Thank you, Lord, for making us thankful. We thank
you for life itself; for the energy your passion for creation gives us; for friendships through which we discover
our lives; for love and lust that remind us we are bodies;
for that body called the church, where our bodies are
enlarged; for the Eucharist, the great thanksgiving, in
which we are made part of your redemption. For all
this we thank you. Amen. (Hauerwas, *Prayers Plainly
Spoken*, 97)

QUESTIONS FOR REFLECTION
AND APPLICATION

1. What does it shift for you to consider Paul's co-writers
   when you study his letters?

2. When you see the link in Greek between "faith/*pistis*"
   and "believe/*pisteuō*," how does that effect your understanding of salvation and discipleship?

3. How do faith, hope, and love all relate to the gospel?

4. How does good theology work to cultivate good behavior?

5. In what ways do you need God's exodus-like salvation to show up in your life?

FOR FURTHER READING

Matthew W. Bates, *Gospel Allegiance: What Faith in Jesus Misses for Salvation in Christ* (Grand Rapids: Brazos, 2019).

Stanley Hauerwas, *Prayers Plainly Spoken* (Downers Grove: IVP, 1999).

Karl Vaters, *De-sizing the Church: How Church Growth became a Science, Then an Obsession, and What's Next* (Chicago: Moody, 2024).

Tom Wright, *Surprised by Hope: Rethinking Heaven, the Resurrection, and the Mission of the Church* (New York: HarperOne, 2008).

GROWTH IN A CHRIST VISION

Colossians 1:15–20 (reformatted)

[15] *The Son is the image of the invisible God, the firstborn over all creation.* [16] *For in him all things were created: things in heaven and on earth, visible and invisible, whether thrones or powers or rulers or authorities; all things have been created through him and for him.*

> [17] *He is before all things, and in him all things hold together.*

> [18] *And he is the head of the body, the church.*

He is the beginning and the firstborn from among the dead, so that in everything he might have the supremacy. [19] *For God was pleased to have all his fullness dwell in him,* [20] *and through him to reconcile to himself all things, whether things on earth or things in heaven, by making peace through his blood, shed on the cross.*

By most accounts, today's reading was an early Christian hymn. Or, a Christian hymn that Paul edited. Not long after Colossians was written Pliny wrote that the Christians "were in the habit of meeting on a certain fixed day before it was light, when they sang in alternate verses a hymn to Christ as to a god" (Epistles 10.96–97). We cannot be certain today's beautiful poetry was one such early Christian hymn, but we know Paul and Timothy had grown up in a singing faith. The Book of Psalms is all one needs to say. We find the presence of songs in the Dead Sea Scrolls. Jesus and his disciples sang together (Matthew 26:30). But the songs the earliest followers of Jesus grew up singing morphed when they became convinced Jesus was the Messiah. Many think Luke 1–2's poetic lines were songs, and the Book of Revelation has numerous songs in which Jesus is central. In Colossians 3:16 Paul will urge singing as he did in Ephesians (5:19). If someone was assigning early songs to their subject manner, as is done in our hymnbooks, this song in Colossians 1:15–20 would be under the "Jesus Christ" heading.

Indications of a Hymn

According to Ralph Martin, an expert on early Christian hymns, the following are possible indicators of a song, with a comment on whether this indicator can be found in Colossians 1:15–20:

1. Introductory formula (yes; 1:15, 18b begin with a "who"; the NIV drops it)
2. Participles preferred to verbs (not this passage)
3. Unusual themes for the author (yes; e.g., "invisible God" etc.)
4. Narrative break that interrupts (yes)
5. Rhythmical, poetic style (yes)

6. Unusual vocabulary ("firstborn" etc.)
7. Dense theological formulations (yes)
8. Ardor and enthusiasm (harder to determine, but yes)

Ralph Martin, *Carmen Christi*, 2nd ed. (Grand Rapids: Wm. B. Eerdmans, 1983), 19. For a more detailed listing, see Matthew E. Gordley, *New Testament Christological Hymns: Exploring Texts, Contexts, and Significance* (Downers Grove: IVP Academic, 2018), esp. 20–21.

The denseness and sheer brilliance of each line and nearly every word require extensive commentary, but we can only dip into this passage with three observations.

Wisdom Is a Person

Paul and Timothy could not stop themselves after reporting to the Colossians their prayer request for the believers to grow in wisdom (1:9–10). They decide that thanksgiving for them ought to be followed immediately with a song devoted to Christ. The song in today's reading identifies the wisdom of God with Jesus himself. Terms in this song that show up in Jewish wisdom texts include "image" of God, of course words about wisdom like perception and understanding, and creation—its beginning and God holding all creation together. One scholar, John Balchin, summarized wisdom in Judaism like this, and I reformat his words into a list with his summary conclusion at the end:

1. Wisdom originates with God, shares his throne, and was with him from the beginning.

2. Wisdom is the agent of creation, and Providence, as well as revelation.
3. Wisdom both comes and is sent into the world, and even returns to heaven again.
4. Wisdom has a soteriological function in the world.
5. Wisdom seeks out men and women and makes personal claims and promises.
6. Wisdom is associated with the spirit.
7. Wisdom is even the agent of judgment.

All this would fuse together in a new pattern when a real person eventually did emerge whose status and origin could only be described in terms like these, and who may even have laid claim to them himself. (Balchin, "Paul, Wisdom, and Christ," 208–209)

It is that last long sentence that returns us to the song in Colossians: that wisdom is the person Jesus Christ. Those ideas combine with Paul's terms to present Christ as the Wisdom of God and, as the Wisdom of God, Jesus Christ is both Creator and Redeemer. I'm afraid you and I, as moderns, may just not be all that impressed with early Christians identifying Jewish Wisdom with Jesus, but it was a bold, even audacious, claim by them to do so. Jesus is given divine status in his song. Who else creates? Who else redeems? Who else but God!

The irony runs thick: an ordinary-looking Jewish Galilean man who grew up on the lower shelves of society, who had recognizable powers and who could teach in a way that drew attention from everyone, but who was crucified outside the City of Jerusalem as a false claimant to king, and who was claimed to have been raised from the dead, is here identified as Creator and Redeemer of all things.

Wisdom Creates

Having prayed for wisdom and given thanks for God the Father liberating and relocating those in Christ, Paul and Timothy delve into Christ as Creator (1:15–17). The Son is the "image of the invisible God," which means Adam and Eve were copies of Jesus Christ (Genesis 1:26–27). The One who was previously invisible (God) becomes visible (Jesus Christ). To this the song adds "the firstborn over all creation," and the "over" comes from the meaning of "first-born" because it has the sense of preeminence and rank, as in Colossians 1:18 ("the supremacy"), and much less emphasis on the "born" part of firstborn (MacDonald, *Colossians*, 58–59). Jesus, then, is not one of the created ones. He is over all creation.

Verse sixteen clarifies any questions one might have: "all things were created . . . in him," with the language the same as the "in Christ" formula (1:2, 4, 16, 17, 19, 28; 2:5, 6, 7, 9, 10, 11, 17). If Christ created all things, Christ is not created. Again, a remarkable claim. The "all things" are detailed in 1:16 to include whatever exists in both heaven and earth, whatever is visible or invisible, and all the various levels and patterns of government, both earthly and spiritual. Which means Christ is responsible for the creation of even the spirits, who were of course created good but at some time turned against the ways of their Creator.

All things were created "through him," which repeats that Jesus is the Creator, but the song adds another expression: all things were created "for" him (1:16). The "for" expresses direction. That is, Christ created all things to reflect honor and praise and glory back to Christ as their Creator. The awe and immensity we sense as we experience the ocean, the vastness of forests, and the immensity of the sky may be seen as an experience of the divine, which it is, but Paul and

Timothy teach the Colossians that the divine we experience is Christ the Creator.

The first "stanza" of this song ends with a final line that summarizes Christ as Creator: "He is before all things, and in him all things hold together" (1:17). He is not part of that creation; he ante-dates all creation. In fact, creation rolls onward in its rhythms and orders and glories and vastness *as an ongoing, sustaining, and intentional act by Jesus Christ.* He prevents creation from returning to its original disorder (Genesis 1:2).

Ellen Davis reminds us, or informs us, that "deep ecologists" (I had not heard of this expression before) "are those who believe that the ecological crisis is not in the first instance a crisis in technology, but rather that the root cause lies in the human heart. In a word, deep ecologists believe that the ecological crisis stems from what Christians call 'sin,' above all the sin of isolating ourselves from the rest of creatures, preferring the immediate advantage of the privileges of our species over the well-being of all creation. Conversely, deep ecologists believe that humans must reconnect with the rest of the creatures, if this wounded yet still lovely planet is to be a livable place for us all" (Davis, *Preaching the Luminous Word*, 301–302). She said these words one time when she was preaching about today's text.

In today's reading Christ is the Wisdom of God, the Wisdom Creator, and this means Christ has left his imprint on all creation. Believers who see in Christ the embodiment of God's fullness ought to be those who see the imprint of Christ in creation so much that how we treat this world is how we are treating Christ. All creation is related to Christ, and in Christ all creation exists. If we are in Christ, we are "in there" with all creation. Those who believe Jesus is Lord also believe our Jesus is the Lord of all creation. A deep Christology entails a deep ecology!

153

Wisdom Redeems

From creation, Paul and Timothy open a new stanza with a summary line, leading the listeners to words about the Creator Christ as the Redeemer Christ (1:18a). As Redeemer, Christ is the "head of the body" of Christ, the "church." As discussed earlier in this book (Ephesians 1:22; 4:15; 5:22), head is a metaphor in need of sorting. Context determines the sort. In Colossians 1:18, head designates Christ as redeemer by way of his First-ness ("beginning") and his resurrection, the fullness of God indwelling him, and this magnificent work of reconciling all things in his death. As Redeemer, he has the "supremacy" (1:18b). He is the Greatest of all greats, but in this context his headship is one of redeeming (and creating by implication). Ruler he is, but headship has to go with the flow of the evidence, and it flows in the direction of Head-as-Redeemer.

His resurrection makes him the "preeminenting one" (1:18; *Second Testament*), and the translation reflects the ongoingness of Christ's preeminence. He not only became preeminent through his resurrection, but he continues as the preeminent one. Two more major affirmations about Christ follow. The first is the mind-boggler: "Because in him all the fullness was delighted to reside" is the *Second Testament* translation, while the NIV fills in some gaps with "For God was pleased to have all his fullness dwell in him" (1:19). Of course, Colossians 2:9's language gives the NIV permission to fill in those blanks. Our translation leaves 1:19 as it is, and what it is matters. This verse claims the entirety of God's fullness resided and resides in Jesus Christ. Amazing. Margaret MacDonald speaks for many when she writes, "The fullness refers to the fullness of God in its totality" (MacDonald, *Colossians*, 63). In Christ we see the fullness of God. The fullness of God resides in Christ, not in the sense of occasionally popping through but in the sense that the embodied Jesus Christ, Jesus the Galilean prophet and Messiah, is God, and we know God by viewing Jesus. One well-known scholar was fond of uttering that we are not to assume we know who God is and then see if Jesus matches up to what we think of God. He turned that around to say that we need to ask if our view of Jesus is shaping our view of God! (Wright, *Changing Face*).

As the embodiment of God's fullness, God "through him" was called "to reconcile to himself all things," and here the "all things" are the same as the all-things of creation (1:16, 17). Not only is God's fullness indwelling Christ, but that fullness means the redemption of all creation. That reconciliation, which is:

> making peace between God and people as well as
> between people and people as well as
> between God and people and creation,

occurs through the cross of Jesus Christ (1:20). At the strictly literal level, this song sings about universal redemption. While that may excite the hearts of many, no one in the New Testament believes that redemption occurs (1) apart from Christ's own work of redemption on the cross or (2) apart from faith in Christ. So, wisdom leads us to affirm the expansiveness of Christ's redemption as the intent of this song while that expansiveness makes room for some opting out or, if you prefer, never having opted in.

We now need to pause only briefly to state why it is that Paul and Timothy included this rich, dense, and evocative song: *because if you get your ideas about Christ right you can ward off bad ideas and go on to good practices and behaviors.* Which is what Paul and Timothy do in the rest of this letter. Including this song will lead Colossians back into the proper ideas when they gather to worship God who became visible in Christ.

QUESTIONS FOR REFLECTION
AND APPLICATION

1. How does Jesus represent the culmination of wisdom?

2. What stands out to you as most important in this reflection on Christ as creator?

3. Why should an understanding of Christ as creator impact our work on ecology?

4. Is your view of Jesus shaping your view of God, or vice versa?

5. How is your view of Jesus shaping your practices and behaviors?

FOR FURTHER READING

John Balchin, "Paul, Wisdom, and Christ," in *Christ the Lord: Studies in Christology Presented to Donald Guthrie*, ed. H.H. Rowdon (Downers Grove: IVP, 1982), 204–219.

Ellen Davis, *Preaching the Luminous Word: Biblical Sermons and Homiletical Essays*, with Austin McIver Dennis (Grand Rapids: Wm. B. Eerdmans, 2016), 301–305.

N.T. Wright, *The Changing Face of God: Lincoln Lectures in Theology, 1996*, Lincoln Studies in Theology (Lincoln, England: Lincoln Cathedral, 1996).

Pliny the Younger, *The Letters of the Younger Pliny*, trans. Betty Radice (London: Penguin, 1969).

GROWTH INTO THE MISSION

Colossians 1:21–2:5
(reformatted)

[21] **Once** you were alienated from God and were enemies in your minds because of your evil behavior. [22] **But now** he has reconciled you by Christ's physical body through death to present you holy in his sight, without blemish and free from accusation—[23a] **if you** continue in your faith, established and firm, and do not move from the hope held out in the gospel.

> [23b] (This is the gospel that you heard and that has been proclaimed to every creature under heaven, and of which I, Paul, have become a servant.)

[24] Now I rejoice in what I am suffering for you, and I fill up in my flesh what is still lacking in regard to Christ's afflictions, for the sake of his body, which is the church. [25] I have become its servant by the commission God gave me to present to you the word of God in its fullness—[26] the mystery that has been kept hidden for ages and generations, but is now disclosed to the Lord's people. [27] To them God has chosen to make known among the Gentiles the glorious riches of this mystery, which is Christ in you, the hope of glory.

²⁸ He is the one we proclaim, admonishing and teaching every-one with all wisdom, so that we may present everyone fully mature in Christ. ²⁹ To this end I strenuously contend with all the energy Christ so powerfully works in me.

²:¹ I want you to know how hard I am contending for you and for those at Laodicea, and for all who have not met me personally. ² My goal is that they may be encouraged in heart and united in love, so that they may have the full riches of complete understanding, in order that they may know the mystery of God, namely, Christ, ³ in whom are hidden all the treasures of wisdom and knowledge. ⁴ I tell you this so that no one may deceive you by fine-sounding arguments. ⁵ For though I am absent from you in body, I am present with you in spirit and delight to see how disciplined you are and how firm your faith in Christ is.

The mission of Paul, who is now personally writing in the first person ("I"—1:23, 24), was to lead gentiles into the presence of God. For gentile converts to be ready for the pres-ence of the God who is altogether holy, they would have to grow in holiness, in their devotion (1:21–23). That is Paul's mission (1:24–2:5). Explaining the mission helps people who need to know. Sometimes the people don't like the mission and leave; other times the people embrace the mission and the work flourishes. Sometimes, unlike Paul, the leaders fail to communicate the mission. Instead, they assume everyone knows. In fact, not everyone knows what the mission is, while most think they know! Which is why Paul provides here a wonderful model: he communicates in the second portion of today's passage a statement of his mission.

The printed text above inserts a parenthesis around 1:23b and sets it off from 1:23a and 1:24. The last word of 1:23a is "gospel," and that word launched Paul into an artic-ulation of his mission, 1:24–2:5, with 1:23b a parenthetical remark. Two parts form in this passage: the first is the story and requirement for the Colossians (1:21–23a) and the second the mission of Paul (1:24–2:5). Paul exhorts the believers to set their lives into the story of what God is doing in the mission.

THEIR STORY

Paul likes the "once-but now" formula because it not only rewrites the personal stories of each believer, but it also reminds them of where they were, where they are, and where they are headed. Their past is broken into two parts: a time of thorough alienation and internal hostility (1:21). We need to expand the sense of "in your minds." The Old Testament's term for heart is often translated with the word translated here as "mind" (*dianoia*), in which case this term indicates one's emotions, passions, and thinking. They were "once othered," and it needs to be noted that the NIV has added "from God" to the alienation, but "from God" is not in the text. Ephesians has a near parallel and there the alienation is from Christ, from God, especially from the people of God, and as well that alienation led to their being engaged in a sinful way of life (Ephesians 2:12; 4:18–19). Being "othered," then, is a wide term about gentiles and their distance from God, from the work of God through the covenant people, from Israel, and this othering was clear in their toxic behaviors. Persons of color, those with disabilities, those with less than adequate economic resources, and those without educational status as measured by those with it, have each been othered in our society. They hear the experience of gentiles as their experience. The dominant culture Christians of our society, even if they are gentiles (and most are), are tempted to skip over the alienation of this text. To do so is to fail the text. The *only* persons in Paul and Timothy's minds who are not alienated are the people of Israel. Everyone else can sit with this text until they see themselves as the othered, as those in need of reconciliation.

Alienation was shaped by both cosmic powers (1:16; 2:8, 15) and by toxic ideas and attitudes, as well as by "evil works" (*Second Testament*). Ephesians details the behaviors: futile thinking, ignorance, darkened understanding, and a hardened heart—"Having lost all sensitivity, they have given themselves over to sensuality so as to indulge in every kind of impurity, and they are full of greed" (Ephesians 4:17–19). All Colossians 1:21 provides is a summary toxicity: "evil works." That was the past of his audience. Then something happened, something inside them and something inside. We have all known such moments and "These moments are precious to us. When they occur it is as though, on the winding ill-lit stairway of our life, we suddenly come across a window, through which we catch sight of another and brighter world—a world to which we belong" (Scruton, *Confessions of a Heretic*, 88).

Their present flips the script. Transformation has taken place. Paul features three new characteristics: *God reconciled them to himself.* They did not engage in a sit-down that led to a peace accord. No, God did it all in Christ (1:13–14, 20). That is, and here I use a literal rendering, "he . . . reconciled in his flesh's body through the death" (*Second Testament*), which the NIV ably translates as "reconciled you by Christ's physical body through death" (1:22). Second, God reconciled them *to prepare them for God's presence,* that is, "to present you holy in his sight, without blemish and free from accusation." But Dennis Edwards summons us into the Now in these words: "when the larger society views you and your people as unclean, blameworthy, and reproachable, as has been the case with African Americans, Paul's words to the Colossians provide spiritual balm to soothe damaged psyches" (Edwards, "Colossians," 487). To turn his insight over, we must admit that whiteness and our dominant culture established that perspective on our brothers and sisters of color. White folks especially are tempted to think of our presentation to God happening in the future at the final judgment. Yes, that's almost certainly the primary connotation, but the presentation is on the basis of a third characteristic: *allegiance.* And allegiance puts us in the here and now. Decker-Lucke reminds us that this language about blemishes and accusations was and is heard differently for women who lived in a culture shaped by and for men and their honor: "Women were in many ways the keepers of the family's honor, and those women who were not able to maintain irreproachable conduct and reputation would bring shame on themselves and their families. Girls and women would have especially understood the importance and relief at being found blameless and irreproachable, free from shame" (Decker-Lucke, "Colossians," 716).

The NIV's rendering is exquisite. It has "—if you continue in your faith" (1:23), or perhaps in "the faith." That em dash (—) provides the condition that they need to remain or continue in their allegiance or in their adherence to the true faith. They will be presented before God as holy *only if* their faith is more than the one-and-done, the faith-only, the nothing-but-faith approach to salvation. True faith is both an initial and an ongoing trust. Faith is allegiance, which transforms a person's walk with Christ into an allegiance that is "established and firm" (1:23). Or, allegiance becomes both "founded and stabilized," like a home built on rock (*Second Testament*; see Matthew 7:24–27). This is not sinlessness, but faithfulness. It is about transformation. I quote from David de Silva again:

> God offers you the means to be reconciled with him
> and to become a new person who will want and love

and do what is pleasing to him because the Spirit of his Son will live in you and *change* you. The result of God's kindness and activity is that you will live a new kind of life now and, after death, live forever with him. (de Silva, *Transformation*, 2)

The allegiant believer, over time, grows in fitness-for-God's-presence so much that, yes, Paul (cf. 1:25, 28) can present them to God as "without blemish and free from accusation" (1:22). Something happens here that transcends even the most transformed believer. No believer is ever spotless, inerrant, or unimpeachable. We have all sinned. No, the idea must be that God purges us from sin in the heat of death and resurrection so that when we come before God the absolute holiness of God recognizes us as fit for the divine encounter and presence. Traditionally Christians have filled in the blanks by saying we are only spotless because we are clothed in the righteousness of the spotless lamb, Jesus Christ. I agree, but that robe fits us because we have been prepared through transformation for the final garment.

Their story then is a "you were" and a "but now you are." Their allegiance is to the hope laid out in the gospel. As I said previously that gospel launched Paul into a description of his mission.

PAUL'S MISSION OF TRANSFORMATION

Paul did not have a self-identity problem, and in fact we might learn from him the insight that shaping our self-identity in Christ can form in us a secure, deeper meaning for life. The direction of Paul's self-identity-shaped mission was not evangelism or planting churches, but the one gospel's transforming powers (1:23b). Paul confesses he is the gospel's servant (the word often transliterated into "deacon"). Notice the shift that occurs at the very end of v. 23 all the way through 2:5: "I" and "me" and "my" highlight the personal (self-identity) nature of this section, with its clear sense of male agency, and he provides for pastoral leaders today a template of pastoral care for people. This personal section emotionally contrasts with the polemics in other personal descriptions of his mission, and the calmer approach here may be because the problem people at Colossae are not personal rivals or opponents of Paul (see for contrast Galatians 1:15–17; 2:7–9; esp. 2 Corinthians 10–13).

First, he suffers, and what he says here has been abundantly confusing in the history of interpretation. What looks like simple terms reads like this: "I now rejoice in the sufferings for you and I fill up the lacks and Christos's troubles in my flesh for his body, which is the assembly [church]" (1:24; *Second Testament*). Hoo boy, this is a hard one. Paul seems to suggest he's completing what Christ left incomplete. Let's begin, however, with this observation. In this context, Paul is providing a narrative of his sufferings in the context of the gospel narrative, which is a narrative about Jesus. I categorize what I think is the best view as the "missional-Christoformity" approach. "Paul understands his gospel-mission sufferings as an intentional entrance into sufferings of, or like those of, Christ, and again like Christ, he suffers for the benefit of the church the more Christoform he becomes; furthermore, he understands his suffering as experiencing the fire *instead of* and *for the benefit of* the Colossians" (McKnight, *Colossians*, 189–190). Both Philippians 3:10–11 and 2 Timothy 2:8–12 are the best explanation of Colossians 1:24, so I quote 2 Timothy:

> Remember Jesus Christ, raised from the dead, descended from David. This is my gospel, for which I am suffering

even to the point of being chained like a criminal. But God's word is not chained. Therefore I endure everything for the sake of the elect, that they too may obtain the salvation that is in Christ Jesus, with eternal glory. Here is a trustworthy saying:

> If we died with him,
>> we will also live with him;
> if we endure,
>> we will also reign with him.
> If we disown him,
>> he will also disown us.
>
> (2 Timothy 2:8–12)

Paul only completes what Christ suffered because Christ died and has been raised. Paul, and all others suffering for the gospel, are finishing off the sufferings of Christ because they enter into and participate in his previous suffering. Anyway, Paul's sufferings, unlike Christ's, do not provide salvation. But, his sufferings benefit others, namely, the Colossians!

Second, he presents people to God. His mission is not about his own glory; it is about leading others into the presence of God. As mentioned above, it was not entirely clear who was doing the presenting at 1:22. I said it was probably Paul. Verses twenty-five and twenty-eight make it clear that Paul as well as Timothy are presenting them to God as mature. Parents, pastors, and spiritual directors—and others—assume (the biblical notion of) a burden for the transformation of others. Those in their care are of course responsible, too, but Paul and Timothy know their calling is gospel transformation, not just gospel proclamation. The presentation element of caring for others includes praying for them, counseling them, guiding them, and most especially loving them by being with them, for them, and growing alongside them.

Third, he gospels. I have for decades taught seminary students, most of whom are pastoring while others are thinking about pastoring someday. Some think their primary task is the Sunday AM sermon, or in those bigger churches, Saturday evening and Sunday AM sermons. Paul gospels, but his terms about preaching are richer than what we call a sermon. He sees the gospeling task of proclaiming "mentoring every human and teaching every human in all wisdom" (1:28, *Second Testament*). The NIV's "admonishing" strikes me as too narrow, perhaps focusing on correcting. The Greek term envelops the ideas of advising, warning, and guiding—all in one. The word "mentoring" captures it well. Teaching, too, is involved in proclaiming. Proclaimers who both mentor and teach are people who listen, converse, discuss, and instruct. The tendency to go all didactic on the audience does not capture what Paul and Timothy think they are called to do. A strong term at work in the gospeling feature is to "contend" (1:29; 2:1). The image of competing with other ideas, with deconstructing toxic ideas, of establishing better and truer ideas—these are at work in the contest Paul has entered.

The best way to participate in the gospel transformation contest is by providing a better story than the alternatives. Polemics, arguments, and public debates on social media are the worst approaches. At times we have to disagree, but the more often we can contest bad ideas with good ideas the better. That contest pops up again in 2:4. Evidently some bandy about with some toxic ideas that deceive and appear in "fine-sounding" or persuasive words. I opened a small package with a book in it recently, sent to me by the author. What struck me about the book was that *everyone else in the entire world—Catholics and Protestants—was wrong and this person was right*. Those are the sorts of teachers and preachers who require our alertness. Paul and Timothy occasionally encountered teachers who had some crazy ideas, and we will meet them in our reflections on 2:8, 16–19, 20–23. We can wait for those reflections.

Fourth, he encourages even those who have never met him. "My goal," Paul says, "is that they may be encouraged in heart and united in love" (2:2). These words are shaped for the believers he has not met in Laodicea, and probably for the Colossians (and those in Hierapolis), the churches planted by Epaphras in the Lycus Valley of western Asia Minor. His aim for them is the aim for the Colossians (cf. 2:2–3 with 1:9).

Fifth, he is present with them "in the Spirit" (2:5), with the possibility that he means something more general, as in the NIV's "in spirit." Distinguishing between the divine Spirit and the human spirit, however, is not as easy as one might think (Levison, *Seven Secrets*). I think Paul means "Spirit" and not "spirit," but either way Paul wants them to know that he is present with them, that he is hearing about the spiritual discipline, and about the firmness of their allegiance in Christ (2:5).

Whatever we say about Paul's mission in the transformation of gentiles, we can say that he knew what God had called him to do. His robust self-identity allowed him to avoid useless, self-defeating comparisons with others. As David Pao writes, "In our contemporary culture, where greatness is often defined by one's popularity, income, or social and political status, this section serves as a powerful reminder for the church to create a different culture, where significance is to be measured in a radically different way. . . . For us, our identity and worth are to be measured by our faithfulness to God's wider plan of redemption and our specific calls within that plan" (Pao, *Colossians*, 143).

Questions for Reflection and Application

1. How does it feel to see yourself as among the "othered" in Paul and Timothy's letter?

2. How does Paul's "once-but now" construction help highlight the transformation that Jesus works in people's lives?

3. On the once-but now formula, read 1 Corinthians 6:9–11, Romans 5:8–11, and 1 Peter 2:10, 25 as well as Hebrews 12:26. Make a list of what marked the past and what marks the present.

4. What does it mean for true faith to be both initial and ongoing?

5. Have you, like Paul, felt a burden and taken on suffering for the transformation of others? What was that experience like?

FOR FURTHER READING

David de Silva, *Transformation: The Heart of Paul's Gospel* (Bellingham, Washington: Lexham, 2014).

Jack Levison, *Seven Secrets of the Spirit-Filled Life: Daily Renewal, Purpose and Joy When You Partner with the Holy Spirit* (Minneapolis: Chosen [Baker], 2023). His ideas about human spirit and the divine Spirit are worked out extensively in a number of books he has written.

Roger Scruton, *Confessions of a Heretic: Selected Essays* (Honiton, Devon: Notting Hill, 2016).

GROWTH IN CHRIST

Colossians 2:6–15

6 So then, just as you received Christ Jesus as Lord, continue to live your lives in him, 7 rooted and built up in him, strengthened in the faith as you were taught, and overflowing with thankfulness.

8 See to it that no one takes you captive through hollow and deceptive philosophy, which depends on human tradition and the elemental spiritual forces of this world rather than on Christ.

9 For in Christ all the fullness of the Deity lives in bodily form, 10 and in Christ you have been brought to fullness. He is the head over every power and authority. 11 In him you were also circumcised with a circumcision not performed by human hands. Your whole self ruled by the flesh was put off when you were circumcised by Christ, 12 having been buried with him in baptism, in which you were also raised with him through your faith in the working of God, who raised him from the dead.

13 When you were dead in your sins and in the uncircumcision of your flesh, God made you alive with Christ. He forgave us all our sins, 14 having canceled the charge of our legal indebtedness, which stood against us and condemned us; he has taken it away, nailing it to the cross. 15 And having disarmed the powers and authorities, he made a public spectacle of them, triumphing over them by the cross.

S he was an influential leader of a large church when she entered seminary and, one day, my office. She had told her story as a part of a paper, and in my office, she told me more of it. She grew up outside the faith. She was very successful in schooling, got a solid degree at a university, and then earned a law degree. Her law career skyrocketed at about the pace her moral life plummeted. She provided details only to turn them into the polar opposite of what her life was like now. Her faith was deep, her spiritual formation intentionally developing, and she combined a clear-window transparency with a humility that eschewed any self-congratulation or self-promotion. When she spoke, her classmates listened. She didn't speak very often. It was as if she had learned to live by James' "be quick to listen, slow to speak" (James 1:19). When she left my office that day, I had experienced a transformed person. You can read some of her story in her book, *Holy Vulnerability* (Fabian), where she introduces us to her themes in these words about Jesus: he "took great care to seek out the broken in body and mind. He looked for those who had no honor, the ones who were shamed because of their social position or physical condition. He met at night with the afraid. He had eyes to see and words to share with the anxiety-ridden. . . . in fact, have you ever noticed how the spiritual elite of Jesus' day didn't really like him, primarily because he hung around people like us? You know, the broken, ashamed, anxious, and afraid" (Fabian, *Holy Vulnerability*, 3). The ones for whom grace and growth matter.

Both Ephesians and Colossians are shaped by themes about grace and growth in unity with Christ and with one another. God's grace to us in Christ redeems but the kind of redemption grace performs is one that leads to growth and transformation. Paul and Timothy are not theoretical theologians. They are pastors of people, so the themes about grace and growing lead them to talk about the personal transformations of the Colossians themselves. In today's reading, the work of God in Christ and the transformation of life among the Colossians are beautifully intertwined.

LIVING IN CHRIST

Colossians 2:6–7 puts into compact words the essence of the Christian life for Paul and Timothy. Many today have made it their life verse(s). Why? For these reasons:

1. The beginning of a confession of Jesus as Lord connects to present living.
2. Faithfulness to Christ is the essential summons: "continue to live."
3. The entire Christian life is rooted in, and formed upon or growing out of, Christ.
4. Being "assured in the faith" strengthens our faith (*Second Testament*).
5. All this prompts the attitude of gratitude.

The only flourishing Christian life is one lived in and out of our grace relationship with Christ, and in and out of our participation in his life, death, and resurrection (2:11–12).

Taking the term "rooted" as our idea, the image Paul and Timothy depict for the Colossians is a plant. As the *First Nations Version* puts it, "Let your roots grow deep in him" (2:7). I will choose one of Kris's and my favorite plants: Morning Light decorative grasses. I'm not an arborist, so forgive any misdemeanors in my language. We planted about fifteen of these grasses on a rainy evening about a decade ago. (We found them on sale.) They were tall, thin, and wispy that first year. What we did not know is that our soil is a perfect match and that the new growth each year expands the perimeter of the forming root ball. Nor did we know they would grow to about five or six feet tall, nor that the ball of roots would become about two feet wide. That their long grasses would blow gently in the winds, that their dew-damped blades would gloriously shimmer in the morning sun, and that out of nowhere they would shoot up a head of seeds in a deep maroon each fall. What is undeniable is that attempting to shove a shovel through the root ball requires more strength than I care to muster. (That's an unmanly admission of failure.) Together, these grasses form a fence row of beauty. Together they put Colossians 2:6–7 into an image: "rooted in him." You are aware, of course, that we don't see the roots. What we see is the power of healthy roots nurturing the grasses.

RESISTING TOXIC IDEAS

In verse eight we encounter the first direct description of the problem Epaphras must have faced in Colossae. My suspicion is that Epaphras got in touch with Paul because the problem people in the community were over Epaphras's head. Paul and Timothy (who, as a native not far from Colossae, may have been quite familiar with the kinds of problems Epaphras was facing) laid some foundations already in this letter. In fact, many studies on Colossians see Paul and Timothy responding to the problems in chapters one and two (e.g., 9, 11, 15–20, 21–23, 26–27, 28, 29; 2:1, 2–3, and 2:6–7). We will encounter more of the local toxic ideas in 2:16, 18, 20–23. Most leaders who have experienced toxic teachers would use the term "deception." Toxic ideas are useless if they are not attractive, but attractive can also be deceptive. "Many of us," David Pao writes, "hunger more for things, success, security, and position than we do for God" (Pao, *Colossians*, 175). He's right, and in this hunger, we are connected tightly to the Colossians. The intoxicating abundance of things deceptively rob us of a desire for spiritual satisfaction.

In Colossae there was a Torah-based Jewish-Christian "group of teachers advocating an asceticism designed to lead worshippers into ecstatic, sensory, and mystical experiences," and these experiences were believed capable of conquering the elemental spirits they feared (McKnight, *Colossians*, 32).* This group's broth of attraction was that it creatively combined the law of Moses with mystical, ecstatic experiences. Eugene Peterson offers wise words: "Paul bluntly calls [these toxic teachers] phonies and cheaters. Persons and movements that hide behind a facade of mystery and secrecy usually are spurious. It is iniquity that hides in the midst of mystery; righteousness has nothing to hide. Christ is the mystery of God, but he is displayed openly. He is the secret of God, but he is that secret made known" (Peterson, *Lights a Lovely Mile*, 89).

With this summary now in view, Paul and Timothy bulldoze this theory with the terms "hollow deceit consistent with humans' conventions, consistent with the Kosmos's categories." Put differently, these "elemental spiritual forces" are their soil and root "rather than" Christ. This mystical approach to the Christian faith gets too much of its nourishment from ideas and practices inconsistent with the gospel. The Colossians experienced these principalities as an invisible power at work in their midst, and the appeal was for them to stand there and resist their powers. Just as Jack Scruton did the powers who wanted to modernize his town, Wycombe. You might have some fun with this story, but you will also experience what it means to fight back against the powers:

---

* For more extensive discussion, see McKnight, *Colossians*, 25–34.

"They" was the name that Jack [Scruton] had always used for the established powers, and it was "they" who were at work beyond the living room window. "They" had begun to demolish the High Street. "They" were going to drive a road across the Rye, an ancient piece of common land that united the town with the River Wye and with the Chiltern woodlands that had provided the beechwood for the famous High Wycombe furniture. "They" had in mind to demolish the old mills and half-timbered shops along the London Road, and to use the scheme to replace the higgledy-piggledy facades of a town that clustered around its market cross like a family of piglets around a sow, with a concrete plaza of which "artistic impressions" already existed in glossy brochures. "They" were going to bring to us citizens of Wycombe, whether we liked it or not and in any case without consulting our wishes in the matter, the full panoply of modernist benefits: wide roads, pedestrian zones, high buildings that would deface the sky and wide glass windows from which the new breed of post-industrial worker could stare over spaces as clean, straight and empty as the mind that surveyed them. "They" had assumed that the residents of Wycombe would prove as docile and disorganized as those of Coventry, Winchester, Reading, Newcastle and every other place that had been turned overnight from an English community to an Antonioni film set. But "they" had reckoned without Jack Scruton, who stood bareheaded on the Rye each Saturday, picking people from the crowd like the Ancient Mariner and not allowing them to proceed without appending their signature to his homespun petition. (Scruton, *Gentle Regrets*, 202–203)

Resisting occurs in those who grow into the fullness of the gospel's power, and this picturesque account can be an icon for us to consider how we might resist the constant cosmic "they," what we often call the "principalities and powers."

The Language of the Toxic Teachers

We can't be sure, but the following terms in today's passage almost certainly were those used by the problematic teachers in Colossae. Paul and Timothy grab some of their terms and turn them into Christian ideas. The terms are "philosophy," "elemental spiritual forces," "fullness," "power and authority," "circumcision," "the flesh was put off," and "legal indebtedness."

EMBRACING CHRIST

The answer to the mystics at Colossae was Christ. Their toxic ideas supplanted Christ. The "fullness," which is what the mystics were seeking experientially, "of the Deity" resides "in bodily form" not in their asceticism or mysticism or spiritual practices, but "in Christ" (2:9). As God indwells a body (Christ) so the Christian life is embodied in the Colossians (and in you and in me). The indwelling Christ and indwelling Spirit take up residence in us, and through our bodies we witness to the redemptive ways of God in our communities (our social body) and in our churches (the body of Christ). To embrace Christ is to recognize that our bodies matter.

Thus, they tell the Colossians they "have been brought to fullness" already in Christ (2:10). Christ is enough because Christ is the fullness they are searching for. Not only does "all" that fullness dwell in Christ, but Christ is also the "head over all rule and authority," which means the cosmic powers or spirits or fallen angels the Colossians may be fearing have been defeated by Christ. Not only does the fullness of God dwell in Christ, and not only does he rule over all cosmic powers they fear, but "in him" the believers transcended physical circumcision in a spiritual circumcision. Spiritual circumcision refers to their baptism in water, which re-enacts the death and resurrection of Christ and the participation in that death and resurrection in their baptism. It appears that circumcision, a concrete act on the male's body, was an identity marker the Colossians found religiously meaningful.

The answer, then, to their fear of the cosmic powers and the quest for spiritual, religious satisfaction is Christ—in whom they can find God in the flesh, victory over the powers, forgiveness of sins, and empowerment for living. Toxic theologies have haunted the church since it was founded. Whether we want to point fingers at the health-and-wealth gospel, or the idolatries of Christian nationalism, or the sectarianism of pastor-quacks who develop secrets and mysteries of how to re-explain the Christian life or Christian truth, we can at least connect in some ways with the challenges of the Colossians. What has not changed is the adequacy and sufficiency of Jesus Christ as the incarnation and revelation of God. To be a Christian is to center Jesus Christ in our hearts, minds, and bodies.

LIVING YOUR STORY

Paul and Timothy began today's reading with the essence of the Christian life, dipped the readers into the problems they were facing, reminded them to make Christ the center, and then they took them straight back to the pattern of their own conversions (2:13–15), which echoes 1:21–23. They were once dead but now they are alive. Again, this is all in Christ. And we cannot expect those who do eventually turn to this gospel to be excited about the gospel the first time or the fiftieth time they hear about Jesus. Pastor Frederick Buechner, speaking from a deep well of experience with resisters, once wrote, "So what if even in his sin the slob is loved and forgiven when the very mark and substance of his sin and of his slobbery is that he keeps turning down the love and forgiveness because he either doesn't believe them or doesn't want them or just doesn't give a damn? In answer, the news of the Gospel is that extraordinary things happen to him just as in fairy tales extraordinary things happen" (Buechner, *Telling the Truth*, 7). Or so what if someone is ashamed, anxious, and afraid? Is not God's grace sufficient for us to grow in the midst and sometimes straight out of these?

Now to that extraordinary thing. Shifting from "you" (2:13) to "we/us," they tell the Colossians that this life-giving creative work of God "forgave us all our sins" by "wiping out the handwritten bill," or IOU, "that was against us (with its rulings), which was opposed to us, and he lifted it [the bill] from the midst, nailing it to the cross." The IOU is the impact of the toxic teachers' demand to follow specific practices, and we will discover those in 2:16, 18, 20. Not only did the cross cancel those debts, but that very cross also stripped the cosmic powers at work in them, and that same cross "exposed [them] with frankness"! (2:13–15; *Second Testament*). There is a sweet irony here (D. Edwards, "Colossians," 490): Jesus was himself shamed in a public crucifixion, but Paul turns that inside-out by saying Jesus shamed those who crucified him, and "those" are the cosmic powers at work in this world against the truth of God.

To sum up: the Colossians need not fear the cosmic powers because they have been defeated; they need not worry about the observances demanded by the opponents because they have been taken care of; they need not pursue higher living either through the Torah or with mystical experiences because *Christ is all they need: he is in all and they are in him.* The essence of the Christian life, then, is growing more and more into the absolute adequacy of Jesus Christ.

QUESTIONS FOR REFLECTION AND APPLICATION

1. What does it mean to live a Christian life in and out of a grace relationship with Jesus?

2. What happens when people get rooted in toxic teachings instead of in Christ?

3. What do you find significant about the fact that redemption must include growth and transformation?

4. What spiritual practices can (and at times do) replace Christ?

5. What identity markers in your culture provide religious meaning and satisfaction?

FOR FURTHER READING

Frederick Buechner, *Telling the Truth: The Gospel as Tragedy, Comedy, and Fairy Tale* (San Francisco: Harper & Row, 1977).

Kellye Fabian, *Holy Vulnerability: Spiritual Practices for the Broken, Ashamed, Anxious, and Afraid* (Colorado Springs: NavPress in alliance with Tyndale, 2021).

Eugene Peterson, *Lights a Lovely Mile: Collected Sermons of the Church Year* (Colorado Springs: WaterBrook, 2023).

Roger Scruton, *Gentle Regrets: Thoughts from a Life* (London: Continuum, 2005).

GROWTH IN DISCERNMENT

Colossians 2:16–23

[16] *Therefore do not let anyone judge you by what you eat or drink, or with regard to a religious festival, a New Moon celebration or a Sabbath day.* [17] *These are a shadow of the things that were to come; the reality, however, is found in Christ.*

[18] *Do not let anyone who delights in false humility and the worship of angels disqualify you. Such a person also goes into great detail about what they have seen; they are puffed up with idle notions by their unspiritual mind.* [19] *They have lost connection with the head, from whom the whole body, supported and held together by its ligaments and sinews, grows as God causes it to grow.*

[20] *Since you died with Christ to the elemental spiritual forces of this world, why, as though you still belonged to the world, do you submit to its rules:* [21] *"Do not handle! Do not taste! Do not touch!"?* [22] *These rules, which have to do with things that are all destined to perish with use, are based on merely human commands and teachings.* [23] *Such regulations indeed have an appearance of wisdom, with their self-imposed worship, their false humility and their harsh treatment of the body, but they lack any value in restraining sensual indulgence.*

Two approaches to describing the views of others are not hard to find. One is a discipline, and the other is a temptation. One describes fairly, objectively, and analytically. And to the satisfaction of the one being described. The other labels boldly, subjectively, and polemically. And to the dissatisfaction of the one being described. Since it's always election season in the USA, I indulge. One party describes the other party no more fairly than the other describes it. Even our news media, which have traditionally been required to be objective and even disinterested, have chosen the second approach. But, sad to say, even coffee with friends is spilled when one attempts to be fair-minded about the other party's platform or candidate(s). It is hard to find a conversation in which two persons or more can describe where they agree and where they disagree with a candidate. (Can I get a show of hands of those who think this can be done without snarls or worse?)

If you move from political parties into religions, even the pretense of disinterested description is ditched. Labels become the lingo. Listening to a proponent describe an opponent with labels tells us as much about the proponent as the opponent. However, even with such a lingo, in most cases the proponent's labels reveal something genuine at work in the opponent. In today's passage, Paul and Timothy urge the Colossians to grow in their discernment of the toxic ideas that challenge the Christian community. Our authors prohibit three behaviors (2:16, 18, 21), but they especially name the toxic practices and then evaluate the toxicity (2:16–17, 18–19, 20–23). For this reflection, we will begin with the statements, move to the evaluations, and then finally turn to the three prohibitions. There is no disinterested description by our authors, so we need to keep that in mind.

TOXIC PRACTICES

Many today think the specific practices of this alternative form of worship derive from combining the gospel with a law-based asceticism and mysticism. I say law-based because the practices named in 2:16 are interpretations of the law of Moses: "what you eat or drink, or with regard to a religious festival, a New Moon celebration or a Sabbath day." The last two practices clue us into some form of Judaism, and this leads us to think of kosher food laws. The toxic party may have at least required gentile believers to observe specific requirements for gentiles in the law (cf. Leviticus 17:10–14; 18:6–18, 26).

The next clue about the practices tempting the Colossians reveals these practices are done to achieve experiences. Our authors describe, or label them, as "false humility," which leans in the direction of asceticism (see 2:23), and the "worship of angels," which is not entirely clear. It could mean they worship angels or, more likely, it means "angel-like worship" (*Second Testament*) and, with their going into "great detail about what they have seen," it suggests mystical encounters. Hence, we combine gentiles observing the law in a rigorous fashion so that it leads to ecstatic experiences and visions. Perhaps their exemplar for this form of worship was Moses who, according to a first century Jewish interpreter of the law, Philo, "was an incorporeal hearer of [heaven's endlessly beautiful] melodies, when he went for forty days, and an equal number of nights, without at all touching any bread or any water" (Philo, *On Dreams* 1.36). I have had folks inform me that after they went on an extreme fasting bender, they had some visionary experiences. My doctor friend told me their experiences were brain chemistry.

Finally, we turn to what is mentioned in verse twenty-one, and there what is prohibited by the opponents has to do with not touching something sacred, as in Exodus 19:12, Leviticus 5:3, or 2 Corinthians 6:17, or perhaps touching was a euphemism for sexual relations (1 Corinthians 7:1). Added to not touching, Paul and Timothy remind them that these false teachers also demand not tasting something, which again leads us to think of food laws (as in Colossians 2:16).

What sounds like bizarre practices and beliefs to our contemporaries may strike a connection with those who have participated in specific groups of charismatics and Pentecostals. I am not knocking either group in general, but I am suggesting that the extreme forms of such groups can advise, require, and approve of only those who have attained specific ecstatic experiences—visions and trances and sensations. Sometimes such groups require extensive, body-denying (and unhealthy) fasting feats, as well as the repetition over and over of unusual words. One of my Pentecostal students, who was having fun with his own tribe, said they learned to speak in tongues by saying over and over this: "woulda-coulda-shoulda-boughta-honda." Such practices have at times led to tongues, or even to ecstasies. I'll drop the discussion there.

EVALUATING TOXICITY

Paul and Timothy were not objective, disinterested describers of the problem-people in Colossae. What they knew came from Epaphras, who would have communicated the details. Here are their evaluations:

These are a shadow of the things that were to come; the reality, however, is found in Christ. (2:17)

False humility . . . puffed up with idle notions by their unspiritual mind. (2:18)

They have lost connection with the head [Christ]. (2:19)

. . . elemental spiritual forces of this world (2:20; cf. 2:8) . . . . Destined to perish with use, are based on merely human commands and teachings. (2:22)

. . . an appearance of wisdom, with their self-imposed worship, their false humility and their harsh treatment of the body, but they lack any value in restraining sensual indulgence. (2:23)

That's a gaggle of what strikes us as goofy ideas, but we are not first century Colossians. We should then check our snarls and eye rolls and pretentious high places and seek to understand that these Colossians, however mistaken, were zealous for the kind of religious worship that could check "sensual indulgence." Again, this all suggests rigorous ascetic practices developed to defeat the flesh, whether sexual or otherwise (1 Corinthians 7; 1 Timothy 4:3). At the heart of the Colossian problem was the human, physical body. The toxic teaching contended the body could be overcome with rigorous ascetic practices. For Paul and Timothy, the body has been transformed in Christ and should no longer be the problem (Colossians 2:12–13; 3:1–4).

Paul and Timothy will have none of it, and so they label the toxic ideas with harsh terms, the most important of which is that those following the toxic leaders have cut themselves off from the adequacy and sufficiency of Christ (1:13–14, 15–20, 27; 2:3, 9–15). If they are right about this splitting away from Christ, all the other terms become pastorally appropriate, even if they are harsh and boundary-forming. Whatever takes us away from the sufficiency of Christ deserves to be dumped. Which is why Paul and Timothy have two, or three, prohibitions.

PROHIBITIONS

The first prohibition exhorts the Colossians not to let the toxic teachers "judge" them, and this has the sense of condemning in an ultimate sense (2:16). By the time we reach maturity we have encountered someone, somewhere who questions our salvation because we believe this or that, or don't believe this or that, or practice or don't practice this or that. The first time I encountered this, when I was about twenty years old, someone called me into question because I had never spoken in tongues, which that person claimed was the necessary sign of the indwelling of the Spirit. Even if I later learned that most charismatics did not agree with this contestant of mine, I did a double-take and studied the Bible harder on the question and determined the Bible didn't support my questioner. My contestant, yours, or the Colossians', however, each claim their view as so right that without subscribing to it one's salvation is in jeopardy.

The second prohibition intensifies the first (2:18). This time the toxic teachers are somehow "disqualifying" the Colossians, and again this sounds like claiming they are not saved or have not reached a sufficient level of spirituality to be approved. The term behind "disqualify" is *katabrabeuō*, with the *brabeuō* part coming from umpires awarding prizes for winners in a contest, and then also for those who evaluate, preside, and decide. The *kata* part turns the evaluation negative. Thus, condemn or disqualify or rule against. The basis for disqualifying the Colossians is their own ecstasy and experience, giving off the snobbish sense that they are religious superiors. Paul and Timothy spare no heat in their accusations of arrogance (2:18, 22–23). They're fakes, they're fraudulent, they're false teachers. Paul and Timothy poke their puffy outfits with the pin of pointed propositions.

The third prohibition is actually a question that implies a don't-do-this: "Why," they ask the Colossians, "do you submit" to the rules and regs of these toxic leaders when you already know you have gained the victory over the powers and the systems and the sins by dying and being raised with Christ? This question takes us back once again to 2:9–13 where their baptism into Christ was a participation in the death and resurrection of Christ.

Here our authors provide a powerful tool for growing in discernment of toxic teachings and teachers. They have a habit of judging and evaluating everyone. Their standards are their human-shaped interpretations. Their goal is the ultimate goal of spiritual ecstasy and utter satisfaction. Their methods are rigorous and require deep commitments. Failing to reach the ecstasy is the person's fault, not their teaching. Their promise is victory over sin and dissatisfaction. And the tell-tale sign of their toxic teachings is marginal space given to Jesus as a person and to his accomplishments. Today's reading provides a question for growing in discernment: Is Jesus at the center, or is Jesus but an agent for their teachings? One can ask oneself, Who is getting all the attention in this group? The stunning line of today's reading is found in verse nineteen: "They have lost connection with the head."

The wise stay away from toxic teachers and teaching. The wise stick with those who stick with Christ.

QUESTIONS FOR REFLECTION AND APPLICATION

1. What do you observe about the rhetorical devices Paul and Timothy use to talk about these toxic teachers and teachings?

2. How does Christ's transformation of human lives and bodies help defeat ascetic teachings?

3. Why do you think toxic teachings can draw Christians away from the victory they have in Christ alone?

4. What is your view on ecstatic or ascetic experiences in the Christian life?

5. How can checking for Jesus at the center help you discern toxic teachings you are exposed to?

FOR FURTHER READING

Philo, *On Dreams*, Loeb Classical Library, vol. 5.
Trans. F.H. Colson, G.H. Whitaker (New York:
Harvard University Press, 1968).

GROWTH WITH ONE ANOTHER

Colossians 3:1–17

¹ Since, then, you have been raised with Christ, set your hearts on things above, where Christ is, seated at the right hand of God. ² Set your minds on things above, not on earthly things. ³ For you died, and your life is now hidden with Christ in God. ⁴ When Christ, who is your life, appears, then you also will appear with him in glory.

⁵ Put to death, therefore, whatever belongs to your earthly nature: sexual immorality, impurity, lust, evil desires and greed, which is idolatry. ⁶ Because of these, the wrath of God is coming. ⁷ You used to walk in these ways, in the life you once lived. ⁸ But now you must also rid yourselves of all such things as these: anger, rage, malice, slander, and filthy language from your lips. ⁹ Do not lie to each other, since you have taken off your old self with its practices ¹⁰ and have put on the new self, which is being renewed in knowledge in the image of its Creator. ¹¹ Here there is no Gentile or Jew, circumcised or uncircumcised, barbarian, Scythian, slave or free, but Christ is all, and is in all.

¹² Therefore, as God's chosen people, holy and dearly loved, clothe yourselves with compassion, kindness, humility, gentleness and patience. ¹³ Bear with each other and forgive one another if any of you has a grievance against someone. Forgive as the Lord forgave

you. [14] *And over all these virtues put on love, which binds them all together in perfect unity.*

[15] *Let the peace of Christ rule in your hearts, since as members of one body you were called to peace. And be thankful.* [16] *Let the message of Christ dwell among you richly as you teach and admonish one another with all wisdom through psalms, hymns, and songs from the Spirit, singing to God with gratitude in your hearts.* [17] *And whatever you do, whether in word or deed, do it all in the name of the Lord Jesus, giving thanks to God the Father through him.*

In this letter we are asked to answer a fundamental question that just might stop us in our tracks: Where are you? I could say, *I'm sitting right here in my library at my desk typing out my own answer to that question.* Paul and Timothy would respond to my answer with, *That's not what we mean by "where."* I think I know what Paul would want you and me to answer the question with: *We "are" seated with Christ **at the right hand of God.*** He spells out that answer in Ephesians, too (2:6). It takes an imagination with basketfuls of courage to say *Sitting next to Christ* if someone were to ask you *Where are you?* Even more, it takes even more courage daily to sit with Christ and live in that seat. We want to take a stab at what answering their question with that answer means for us today in this reflection. Before we get there, you might be wondering *Where else? Or, what other location is there?* The answer to that is simple: *On earth. On earth **apart from** Christ. On earth **instead of** rising with Christ.* The on-earth or with-Christ make all the difference in the world for someone who wants to flourish in Christ.

Paul and Timothy contrast the upper and the lower worlds. That upper world is not called "heaven" here. Their terms are "upper," "with Christ," and "at the right hand of God" (3:1), as well as having a life "hidden with Christ in God" (3:3) that they "now" live (3:8) in a "new self" (3:10) or "new human" (*Second Testament*). This map of where we are maps onto how, who we are in Christ, unity with one another develops. And it all begins with "If" (3:1, *Second Testament*) or "Since" (NIV). There is no sense of a "maybe" or "if perhaps" in this "If." It expresses an assumption about which there is no question. But that "IF" transition is a big one because it assumes something theologically true. As Eugene Peterson once put it, "this transition from getting the *story* right to getting our *lives* right" is non-negotiable. He adds that "it is not possible to begin a discussion on Christian living by talking about what we do" (Peterson, *As Kingfishers Catch Fire*, 307, 308). No, we begin with what God has done.

EARTHLY EXISTENCE

In contrast to the upper things, our authors label the lower things as "earthly things" (3:2), as "your earthly nature" (3:5) and, shifting from location to time, "the life you once lived" (3:7) and to elements of who we are in "your old self" (3:9), or the "ancient human" (*Second Testament*). So, the earthly things point to the practices of the life the Colossians lived prior to their conversion to Christ. What comes through this passage loud and clear, even though some have their ears plugged, pertains to a contrast, not between spiritual and physical, and not so much of heavenly and earthly, but between a with-Christ and without-Christ life, a life spilling over in sin or a life spilling over for Christ.

The typical sins of gentiles in the stereotyping mind of a first century Jew like Paul remain constant across Jewish texts. Gentiles partake in "sexual immorality, impurity, lust, evil desires and greed, which is idolatry" (3:5), as well as in "anger, rage, malice, slander, and filthy language from your lips," including lying to one another (3:8, 9). Notice the major themes: sexual sins, greed, and interpersonal relationships.

Exploitation of the bodies of others, a grasping for what others have, and the divisiveness of these sins reveals a fractured society. If there's a more insightful sketch of the sins churches face, I don't know of it. Greed stands out, perhaps. Greed is the desire to acquire more and more, the spirit of consumerism. America's malls and Amazon represent the greed culture because they make more and more available all the time. Those consumed by consumerism, since they constantly indulge in the habits of the thin highs of shallow satisfactions, lose all desire for the future kingdom. They have jettisoned the Christian sense of heaven and eventually lose a heart filled with hope, and hope figures into today's passage (3:4). But Dennis Edwards warns us about turning this passage into a "pie-in-the-sky-when-you-die religion." Any careful reading of this passage will drive us into life in a here-and-now-religion of love, justice, and peace (D. Edwards, "Colossians," 491).

Paul and Timothy both know personally and pastorally that there is a difference between "one" or "then" and the "new" and "where" (1:21, 22; 2:13, 16, 20), and it comes out all over again in today's reading (3:1, 2, 7, 8–10, 12). Those called especially to nurture Christoformity in others know that growth does not happen all at once. One does not become an adult in life at age one, nor does one attain spiritual formation in year one. Christlikeness that removes one from an earthly existence into a Christlike existence requires experience, time, bruises and knock-downs, and encouragement and seeing some progress and learning. It requires examples of those who have walked the walk, and it needs time with mature Christians. A biblical term for this is wisdom. As one who has entered his seventh decade, I am at times stunned by how young leaders can rush to other young leaders, and how they can surround themselves only with young leaders and friends, and how plugged their ears can be to those with wisdom about something (McKnight and Hanlon, *Wise Church*).

WITH CHRIST EXISTENCE

Believers died to the earthly existence in their baptism into Christ (3:3, 5; cf. 2:11–12). Our authors do not develop the theme of death here as was developed in Romans 6. Nor do they appeal to the famous cross-life expressed by Jesus (Mark 8:34–38). But getting beyond our former earthly existence and surrendering to the life with Christ requires death with Christ as much as it requires the power of the resurrection (cf. Colossians 2:10–15). Every day is Easter for the one seated next to Christ.

The alternative to an earthly existence is a life rooted in the resurrection of Christ, and a life of being seated next to Christ. The two previous passages in Colossians about our life "now" pertained to being presented before God and having our sins forgiven (1:21–23; 2:13–14). Today's passage maps the moral life of the one who is undergoing spiritual formation. Their practices include: "set your hearts on things above" and "set your minds on things above" (3:1, 2). The NIV has added "hearts" and "minds" as the human practices pertaining to the upper matters. The Greek texts only have verbs, one with "pursue" and the other with "think" (*Second Testament*).

Their new pursuit is Christ, in whom one's life is hidden (3:3) and who has himself become our very life (3:4). Believers are new people (3:10), and their very existence is being renewed, resulting in a world in which ritual, social status, and ethnic statuses and social divisions carved up human life and assigned people to a class (3:11). Clothing then and now expresses one's identity and social location. Or, as Margaret Atwood writes, "We may not be what we wear, but what we wear is a handy key to who we think we are" (Atwood, *Burning Questions*, 270). That Paul wants them (1) to take off the old and (2) put on a kind of new clothing that expresses (3) interpersonal unity reveals that their new identity and status is in Christ. Daily, we get to wear our "Easter outfit" (Peterson, *Lights Lovely Mile*, 148). David Pao challenges us to think of how the Colossians' new clothing could "externalize their confession under the lordship of Christ" (Pao, *Colossians*, 234).

In this new life, being in Christ is all that matters, and when that kind of life forms it will expose the divisiveness and prejudices of every culture and nation that has ever existed. Equality and equity take root the more time with Christ. The radical nature of this vision appears the moment we take into consideration both the "barbarian" and the "Scythian," the former how Greeks talked about those who could not speak Greek and who were therefore The Other, while the latter is more or less like "hillbilly." The implication of unity in Christ is not erasure of differences but the celebration of diversity. What holds us back and, as an essayist has framed it, is snobbery, which is "the desire for what divides us and the inability to value what unites us" (Epstein, *Snobbery*, 17). Speaking of snobbery, Margaret Atwood just might illustrate it with her putdown: "There is no snobbism quite like French snobbism, especially that of the Left" (Atwood, *Burning Questions*, 403). Again, what keeps us from uniting ethnicities, genders, and social status is snobbery, that life of comparing oneself to others so we end up on the top.

We might ask, as many have, why the famous male-female part of Galatians 3:28 is absent here, in Colossians 3:11, but also in 1 Corinthians 12:13. We can't be sure but there are good reasons to think a neither-male-nor-female concept easily led the early churches into radical, rigorous absence of sexual relations among ascetics (Macdonald, *Colossians*, 146–147). In that Colossians 2:23 clearly worries about rigorous ascetics, I can agree that even minimizing the male-female relation could have led some to rigorous attempts to avoid one of life's deepest pleasures.

The new practices are detailed: "compassion, kindness, humility, gentleness and patience" (3:12), and attending these are virtues like tolerance and forgiveness (3:13). The uppermost virtue, however, is love, and love is the bond that unites and completes all the virtues (3:14). A life marked by these practices leads to peace among one another (3:15), thanksgiving, and mutual nurturing of one another as we sing with one another (3:16). The North Star for this new community shaped by a new self is living every moment "in the name," or a conscious, intentional representing "the Lord Jesus" (3:17). Notice the importance here of singing. Now this comes from my experience in being in churches around the world the last three decades. Some church groups can sing, and some can't. I won't name the ones who can't (or who can but don't unleash the chords), but I can say that charismatics and Pentecostals, non-denominational evangelicals, and Churches of Christ can sing—and Kris and I love to be with those folks when they get to singing.

Notice where these Christian virtues are located: every one of them shows up in interpersonal relations. We may today speak of needing compassion or kindness for ourselves, but the orientation of these virtues is how those in Christ relate to others in Christ, and how that virtue formation works itself into a transformed character so that a believer's treatment of others in the public square now looks different. Too often today we see spirituality as a private matter or as a God-and-me matter, while Jesus and the apostles learned very quickly that genuine spirituality was a relational matter. We are located with Christ in a seat surrounded by innumerable other seats, and as we look to Christ we learn more and more how to interact with others around us.

Christian ethics are fundamentally interpersonal. "Social activism," we are reminded, "is incomplete without spiritual transformation," and spiritual formation is just as incomplete without social activism (D. Edwards, "Colossians," 491). For Paul and Timothy, church life is where one's social life is formed into the common good. It all begins in our location, which requires courage and imagination to comprehend. Eugene Peterson tells such a lovely, imagined story that I want to include it:

> Imagine a young man starting off on a two-mile walk across town to see a girl. Seeing her and spending the evening with her is the purpose and goal of his walk. She is very much alive in his imagination. He can't keep her out of his mind. Passing a delicatessen, he remembers her favorite candy and buys a box. Passing a flower shop, he is inspired with the thought of how lovely she would look with flowers on her shoulder, so he buys a corsage. Passing old acquaintances, he entirely misses even seeing them. Passing a church, he looks particularly long at it, for he once heard her remark that that was where she would like to be married. Nearing her home, he glances at his reflection in a store window, straightens his tie, and fixes his hat. By the time he arrives at her door, we will have been able to list at least a dozen specific actions in the course of the two-mile walk, all caused by the girl in his imagination. She was in his conduct.

Imagine Christ now, and yourself seated next to him. Now we can walk anew, and we can turn from a lovely imagination to a courageous one. Dietrich Bonhoeffer, preaching at the precipice of Hitler's takeover, challenged his congregation to live out the words of Colossians 3:1 about things above and let those words fire up their imagination how best to live in an unjust world falling apart:

> Today, immensely important things will be decided by whether we Christians have strength enough to show the world that we are not dreamers and are not those who walk with their heads in the clouds, that we don't just let things come and go as they are, that our faith is really not the opium that lets us stay content in the midst of an unjust world, but that we, especially because we set our minds on things that are above, only protest all the more tenaciously and resolutely on this earth. Protest with words and actions, in order to lead the way forward at any price. (Bonhoeffer, *Collected Sermons*, 51)

QUESTIONS FOR REFLECTION AND APPLICATION

1. Why is it important to begin discussions of the Christian life with what God has done rather than with what we do?

2. What differences do you see between with-Christ lives and without-Christ lives?

3. Why are older, wise, mature Christians so important in the spiritual development of newer Christians? And vice versa, why is it important for mature Christians to learn from newer Christians?

4. If you consider your location to be "seated next to Christ," what does that make possible for you?

5. Reflect on how what we wear speaks of who we are and where we are on the social ladder. How does today's passage challenge our perceptions of our clothing?

FOR FURTHER READING

Margaret Atwood, *Burning Questions: Essays and Occasional Pieces*, 2004 to 2021 (New York: Doubleday, 2022).

Dietrich Bonhoeffer, *The Collected Sermons of Dietrich Bonhoeffer* (Minneapolis: Fortress, 2012).

Joseph Epstein, *Snobbery: The American Version* (New York: Houghton Mifflin, 2002).

Scot McKnight and Daniel Hanlon, *Wise Church: Forming a Wisdom Culture in Your Local Church* (Eugene, Oregon: Wipf and Stock, 2021). This is a series of chapters written by (mostly) pastors about their need for wisdom in various areas of ministry.

Eugene Peterson, *As Kingfishers Catch Fire: A Conversation on the Ways of God Formed by the Words of God* (Colorado Springs: Waterbrook, 2017).

Eugene Peterson, *Lights a Lovely Mile: Collected Sermons of the Church Year* (Colorado Springs: WaterBrook, 2023).

GROWTH IN CHRIST AT HOME

Colossians 3:18–4:1

18 Wives, submit yourselves to your husbands, as is fitting in the Lord.

19 Husbands, love your wives and do not be harsh with them.

20 Children, obey your parents in everything, for this pleases the Lord.

21 Fathers, do not embitter your children, or they will become discouraged.

22 Slaves, obey your earthly masters in everything; and do it, not only when their eye is on you and to curry their favor, but with sincerity of heart and reverence for the Lord. 23 Whatever you do, work at it with all your heart, as working for the Lord, not for human masters, 24 since you know that you will receive an inheritance from the Lord as a reward. It is the Lord Christ you are serving. 25 Anyone who does wrong will be repaid for their wrongs, and there is no favoritism.

4:1 Masters, provide your slaves with what is right and fair, because you know that you also have a Master in heaven.

Spiritual growth involves the individual person's character taking on glimpses of Jesus himself, but that kind of formation also transforms life in the here and now, beginning in one's home life. It can be disheartening to a person to grow dramatically because of what they have learned from someone, only to learn that that someone was mean as a snake at home or distant from their children or spouse. Growth in spiritual formation that did not impact the household had nothing to do with what Paul and Timothy meant when they wrote "whatever you do . . . do it all in the name of the Lord Jesus" (3:17). Today's reading about the so-called household regulations is about one of those locations for the "whatever" to make an impact.

We must think of the people in Colossae in terms other than complacent souls awaiting the apostle's next directive. The people populating the Pauline churches were personalities, not roles and statuses. Some women were like Mrs. Harling in Willa Cather's *My Ántonia*, who is described in the following terms: "Mrs. Harling was short and square and sturdy-looking, like her house. Every inch of her was charged with an energy that made itself felt the moment she entered a room. Her face was rosy and solid, with bright, twinkling eyes and a stubborn little chin. She was quick to anger, quick to laughter, and jolly from the depths of her soul" (Cather, *My Ántonia*, 112). We tend to treat the personalities in the household regulations in both Ephesians and Colossians as abstract positions on a pole of hierarchical roles. They were lively, vigorous, resourceful, courageous, and in most cases hard-working folks doing what they needed to do to survive. And not always thinking Paul was right.

But, to read today's passage well, we need once again to remind ourselves of the worldview at the time this was written. I repeat, with only slight revisions, here what was written on pp. 107–111.

WORLDVIEW

Aristotle's famous and massively influential book, *Politics*, described and assigned the various roles each person's status was to play in home and society. Paul's order in the household finds a parallel in Aristotle, and this is what Aristotle's looks like:

For husbands and wives: "And since, as we saw, the science of household management has three divisions, one the relation of master to slave, of which we have spoken before, one the paternal relation, and the third the conjugal—for it is a part of the household science to rule over wife and children (over both as over freemen, yet not with the same mode of government, but over the wife to exercise republican government and over the children monarchical); for the male is by nature better fitted to command than the female (except in some cases where their union has been formed contrary to nature) . . . . (1.5.1–2)

For fathers and children: "The rule of the father over the children on the other hand is that of a king; for the male parent is the ruler in virtue both of affection and of seniority, which is characteristic of royal government." (1.5.2)

For masters and slaves: "Since therefore property is a part of a household and the art of acquiring property a part of household management (for without the necessaries even life, as well as the good life, is impossible), and since, just as for the particular arts it would be necessary for the proper tools to be forthcoming if their work is to be accomplished, so also the manager of a household must have his tools, and of tools some are lifeless and others living (for example, for a helmsman the rudder is a lifeless tool and the look-out man a live tool—for an assistant in the arts belongs to the class of tools), so also an article of property is a tool for the purpose of life, and property generally is a collection of tools, and a slave is a live article of property." (1.2.3–4)

If you paid attention to the references in Aristotle's famous book, you will have noticed the numbers are in reverse order. Aristotle began at what he considered the bottom (he called it the "smallest parts") of the household, with the slaves and masters.

Turning to the Jewish world, we can dip into Josephus, a first century Jewish historian, who wrote this about women: "A woman is inferior to a man in all respects" . . . so "let her obey, not that she may be abused, but that she may be ruled" . . . "for God has given power to the man" (*Against Apion*, 201). Josephus, an aristocrat and priest, believed the purpose of sexual relations was procreation (199), that same-sex relations deserved the death penalty (199), and that abortion was to be prohibited (202).

These two thinkers represent well how the household was managed: power was assigned to the head of the household, nearly always a man, and thus can be called patriarchy (which means rule by the father, or the father is first). A strict hierarchy or ordering became intuitive and institutional. This hierarchy reflected status and formed into a superior-inferior order. Put baldly, the ancient world thought women were inferior to men, and slaves were inferior to the free. It has been shown that the Christian church, until the mid-twentieth century, assigned women non-leadership roles *because women were considered inferior* (Witt, *Icons of Christ*). Aristotle and Josephus cannot be seen as ancient authors for their ideas are alive today. Paul cut against their grain, and it is a misfortune of interpretation that his cuts have been smoothed over.

Religion and Marriage

Ryan Burge, one of America's sociologists of religious behaviors, recently posted on his Substack a discussion of a dataset.

> The Association of Religion Data Archives (ARDA) hosts a dataset that is incredibly helpful in this regard. It's called The National Survey of Family Growth (NSFG), and the combined size of the dataset is over 10,000 respondents who were between the ages of 15 and 50 when they took part in the research. It was funded by the Center for Disease Control's National Center for Health Statistics. It asks hundreds of questions of individuals related to topics about marriage and family. It also includes a question about the religious tradition of the respondent.
>
> Some of his conclusions reveal that Christian attempts to "Christianize" the home and marriages is having mixed results in the USA (all bold type is Burge's). Modern Christianizing is especially rooted in the household regulations of Ephesians and Colossians. Evangelicals get married about the same rate as mainliners, while a noticeable difference occurs with African Americans and those with no religion.
>
> A significant portion of this sample is currently married. In many faith traditions, it's about half of respondents including evangelicals, mainline Protestants, and those of

other faith groups like Muslims, Buddhists, and Latter-day Saints. **There were two traditions who were clear outliers here—just 21% of Black Protestants were currently married and it was ten points higher for those with no religious affiliation (31%).** The corollary to that is the share of the sample who had never been married. **The only group where a majority hadn't walked down the aisle were Black Protestants at 56%, while 46% of nones had never been married. The group that was the least likely to never be married were evangelicals at just 31%.**

Teachings against cohabiting, which has been a major fear of the purity culture, and against divorce seem to have little to no impact on evangelicals.

When it comes to the other two options— cohabitating with a partner without being married and being divorced/separated, there isn't a lot of variation. It is noteworthy that across all four Christian categories (evangelical, mainline, Black Protestant, and Catholic) that there was no statistically significant difference in cohabitation rates—they were all between 11% and 13% of the sample. The same is largely true when it comes to divorce and separation. An evangelical was just as likely as a Catholic to select one of these two options.

Ryan Burge: "How Does Religion Influence Decisions about Marriage and Family?" at https://www.graphsaboutreligion.com/p/how-does-religion-influence-decisions.

PERSPECTIVE

People of color in the USA, women, rural Americans, disabled people, and anyone who has been socially marginalized experiences what Paul and Timothy write as a *reinforcement* of unjust social orders. As we read today's passage, we need to keep in mind how these texts have been used against the non-dominant culture. My experience in teaching about the household regulations has been that the following observations are steps toward a radical paradigm shift, both for many today who were nurtured in a complementarian worldview but also for first century Christians.

Each of these points substantively shifts how the household looked for Christians. First, the content and ordering of the household regulations reflect what was commonly believed and said in the world of Paul and Timothy, and that is why they look like they do. Their Greek and Roman audiences would have expected this order, but they would have been stunned at times by what he had to say. Second, in both Ephesians and Colossians *the order is intentionally* flipped: instead of husband-wife, father-children, master-slave, we have wife-husband, children-father, slave-master. They begin, then, with the subordinate and then follows the superordinate. This is unusual, almost unprecedented, and evocative of changes he is making. Third, notice that the superordinate is assumed to have power, *but the instructions diminish the superordinate's power, authority, and thus they prohibit abuses of power.* Aristotle saw the various persons in his hierarchy in terms of ruling over and connected each role to the soul. Here are his words: "Hence there are by nature various classes of rulers and ruled. For the free rules the slave, the male the female, and the man the child in a different way. And all possess the various parts of the soul but possess them in different ways; for the slave has not got the deliberative part at all, and the female has it, but without full authority, while the child has it, but in an undeveloped form" (*Politics*, 1.5.6).

Which leads, then, to fourth: since the power of the superordinate is diminished, the traditional subordinate is *empowered*. Each of the subordinates would have immediately sensed the winds of change. Thus, fifth, the subordinates in each case *are given agency to choose and to take responsibility* in how they related to the superordinate. Paul and Timothy, sixth, expected the subordinates and superordinates to grow into behaviors that were Christian. What is not mentioned here, but which is mentioned in 1 Peter 2:11–3:7, is that the intent of good behavior in the home may be that the early Christians acquire and sustain a good reputation for good citizens, rather than rebellious.

Another observation reveals that what our authors are doing in the household regulations is Christianizing them. The motivations for behaviors are not shaped by the state and its powers (Athens, Rome, Ephesus) but by Christian ethics. Notice "as is fitting in the Lord" (Colossians 3:18), "for this pleases the Lord" (3:20), "but with sincerity of heart and reverence for the Lord" (3:22), "as working for the Lord, not for human masters" (3:23), and both the enslaved and the slaveowners are turned around to face the Lord for their behavior toward one another: "It is the Lord Christ you are serving" (3:24) and "because you know that you also have a Master in heaven" (4:1). A shift in motivation, no matter how helpful it may be to an enslaved person, does not alter social orders. Not until those social orders changed would an appeal to shifting one's motivation be unnecessary. As Dennis Edwards observes in understatement, the fact that God shows no favoritism has not had sufficient impact on Christians themselves (D. Edwards, "Colossians," 495).

A final consideration: these instructions were not timeless, culturally disconnected, abstractions capable of dropping down in all households of all times. While there are some foundational, even timeless principles, appearing here, like "It is the Lord Christ you are serving" (3:24), these are words from Paul and Timothy for a specific context (Colossae) at a specific time (first century) in a particular social context (Roman empire as experienced in Western Asia Minor, in particular, in the city along the Lycus River, Colossae). Understanding how Paul and Timothy advised Christians to conduct themselves in their households can provide insight for how we are to conduct ourselves today in our households. But mark this down: *Had Paul or Timothy lived where you or I live, they would have reframed their teachings and tailored it specifically to our situations.*

INSTRUCTIONS

The language of "submit," which I consistently translate as "order yourselves under" to highlight that the term evokes a social order, is not a do-whatever-the-man-says kind of word. The man involved is a Christian man whose responsibility it is to love one's wife and not be harsh with them (3:18, 19; on love, see pp. 93–94, **early in the passage on Ephesians 5:1–20).** Furthermore, this term is less authoritarian than the term used for children (3:20; "obey"). The mutual submission of Ephesians 5:21, though absent in Colossians, can be assumed on the basis of the mutuality of Colossians 3:12–17. The wife has the agency to choose to order herself in an orderly manner in the home with respect to her husband. Good marriages are formed not by roles in a hierarchy but in a relationship shaped by mutual love. The hierarchies of patriarchalism can at times be conducive to a smooth-working machine but only at the expense of the woman's agency and genuine flourishing.

Household Regulations

The New Testament has several instances of apostles addressing church folks as members of a household. Hence, these passages are called "household regulations," which comes from Martin Luther's German term *Haustafeln*. The following passages illustrate early Christian teaching about life at home:

Ephesians 5:21–6:9
Colossians 3:18–4:1
1 Timothy 2:8–15; 6:1
Titus 2:1–10
1 Peter 2:18–3:7

Children, who are here to be seen and heard and acknowledged to be part of the community of faith, are to listen to, heed, or obey their parents, while the parent in this context, the father, is not to "pick fights with your children" (3:20; *Second Testament*). When our children were young, our daughter kept an immaculate room and our son a, well, less than immaculate room. Once I was irritated with the latter's room and expressed that to Kris, who said, "It's not worth the fight. He'll learn." It was a wise word to a father because it could have led to a damaging battle. It is noteworthy that our authors choose a negative for fathers. Most likely, the negative appears because of the stereotype of authoritative and, at times, authoritarian fathers. Authority acquired does not always mean authority used in love.

The emphasis in this text is on slaves, with words added to the slaveowners, or masters (3:22–4:1). Onesimus was from Colossae, and he may be in mind as Paul and Timothy say what they say (cf. Philemon). As noted earlier in the study of Ephesians, slavery in the Roman world was about status and integrity and identity, all three reshaped by turning a person into a utility. Most slaves were born into slavery, and a slave's life was dependent upon the master's character. A male slave remained in the status of a "boy" his entire life, unless emancipated, in order to prevent a legal marriage, legal control of (their non-legal marital relationship) children, and thus legal inheritance rights. Slaves were commonly abused physically and sexually, and many female slaves were sex slaves to their masters. I want to make two observations, and they will not be comfortable for some. First it is a very, very serious mistake to pretend that slavery then was not the same as slavery in the New World. It's a similar mistake to think of Roman slavery along the lines of modern employment. A slave is an owned body. Furthermore, the word "slave" is a label that devalues a person's dignity, agency, and social status. It is better to say, "enslaved person" than "slave." Second, Paul and his co-workers did not perceive the immorality and hideousness of slavery. As African American New Testament scholar, Dennis Edwards writes, "We cannot help but wonder if Paul's social position as a male Roman citizen obscured his perspectives on vulnerable members of society" (D. Edwards, "Colossians," 494). They swam in waters boiling with slavery and did not perceive they were boiling themselves. There is nothing about this slavery text that transfers into our world easily. Yes, it was beneficial for those who lived in a world of slavery to work in a way that did not get the gospel mission into any more trouble than it already was in. Yes, it is good for people to work for their bosses as people who are serving God and not their bosses, but this text is not about pragmaticism, workers, and bosses but about masters and slaves. It belongs in that world, and I shall leave it there. Paul's teaching here, and elsewhere, has been abused by slaveowners and used to justify violence, rape, and exploitation. American history was (mis)shaped by these verses, and systemic racism names it.

It is reasonable to think the number of lines for the enslaved reflects the number of enslaved in the fellowship in Colossae. The enslaved of the Roman empire depended on the generosity and general good will of their owners. The earliest churches reflect enough of the enslaved in their midst to remind us that they, too, had some agency in what to do with their time. They could, as long as it fit in the schedule of the head of household, attend church gatherings in other homes. Paul and Timothy radicalize their work ethic from the heartless duties of an owned body to the agency and choice of someone who revolutionizes their labor from serving the family to serving the Lord. This is a Christian revolution in the household, even if it was a revolution that did not approach mandated emancipation and liberation. It has been customary, and I know I have done this, to "apply" this passage to employers and employees. I stand again with Dennis Edwards: "interpretations that remove slavery from the context of Paul's words do a further disservice to those who were actually enslaved. Turning Paul's commands into words for how bosses should treat workers is a luxury our enslaved forebears did not have" (D. Edwards, "Colossians," 497).

What is said to the "masters" (NIV) or "lords" (*Second Testament*) in 4:1 is too easily missed. In particular, I strenuously disagree with the NIV's "right and fair" to translate two dynamic words in the first century Christian lexicon: *dikaios* and *isotēs*. The first word evokes justice in that it describes behaviors of a slaveowner that were to be measured by the will of God, not by the best practices, or tolerated customs, of Rome or Colossae. The second term can only mean either equality or, if financial, equity. The NIV's choice of term, "fair," is too casual and misses the radical revolution in the

Christian household. As Paul told Philemon that his slave was now a brother, a sibling, and thus an equal in Christ (Philemon 16), so Paul and Timothy here instruct the slave-owner to treat the enslaved in his care *as an equal.*

The challenge this passage presented to the Colossians was to take Christ home and see what happens when Christ becomes the true head of the household. Today's reading illustrates the earliest Christian experiments with turning one's home into a lab for discipleship. It would take centuries to work this out more intensively, and we still have plenty of room for growth.

QUESTIONS FOR REFLECTION AND APPLICATION

1. Why is the home life of a Christian so important in their discipleship process?

2. How is Paul and Timothy's letter revolutionary for both women and men, especially considering it was written into such a patriarchal context?

3. How does the general principle of Colossians 3:17 manifest itself in 3:18–4:1?

4. Imagine Paul and Timothy's instructions being written to a church near where you live today. What might they say to household members about their family relationships?

5. How can you use authority tempered by love in your relationships? What would you change if you saw Christ as the true head of your household?

FOR FURTHER READING

Aristotle, *Politics*, Loeb Classical Library (Cambridge, Massachusetts: Harvard University Press, 1998) (trans. H. Rackham).

Willa Cather, *My Ántonia*, intro. Lucy Hughes-Hallett, Everyman's Library 228 (New York: Alfred A. Knopf, 1996).

William G. Witt, *Icons of Christ: A Biblical and Systematic Theology for Women's Ordination* (Waco: Baylor University Press, 2021).

GROWTH IN TRANSPARENCY

Colossians 4:2–18

[2] *Devote yourselves to prayer, being watchful and thankful.* [3] *And pray for us, too, that God may open a door for our message, so that we may proclaim the mystery of Christ, for which I am in chains.* [4] *Pray that I may proclaim it clearly, as I should.* [5] *Be wise in the way you act toward outsiders; make the most of every opportunity.* [6] *Let your conversation be always full of grace, seasoned with salt, so that you may know how to answer everyone.*

[7] *Tychicus will tell you all the news about me. He is a dear brother, a faithful minister and fellow servant in the Lord.* [8] *I am sending him to you for the express purpose that you may know about our circumstances and that he may encourage your hearts.* [9] *He is coming with Onesimus, our faithful and dear brother, who is one of you. They will tell you everything that is happening here.*

[10] *My fellow prisoner Aristarchus sends you his greetings, as does Mark, the cousin of Barnabas. (You have received instructions about him; if he comes to you, welcome him.)* [11] *Jesus, who is called Justus, also sends greetings. These are the only Jews among my co-workers for the kingdom of God, and they have proved a comfort to me.* [12] *Epaphras, who is one of you and a servant of Christ Jesus, sends greetings. He is always wrestling in prayer for you, that you*

may stand firm in all the will of God, mature and fully assured.
¹³ I vouch for him that he is working hard for you and for those at
Laodicea and Hierapolis. ¹⁴ Our dear friend Luke, the doctor, and
Demas send greetings. ¹⁵ Give my greetings to the brothers and
sisters at Laodicea, and to Nympha and the church in her house.

¹⁶ After this letter has been read to you, see that it is also read
in the church of the Laodiceans and that you in turn read the letter
from Laodicea.

¹⁷ Tell Archippus: "See to it that you complete the ministry you
have received in the Lord."

¹⁸ I, Paul, write this greeting in my own hand. Remember my
chains. Grace be with you.

The ending of this letter is pure Paul. Pure pastoral, caring, nurturing, and instructing Paul. The Paul we meet in the ends of letters is the same Paul every time, and that Paul is the same Paul one would meet in homes as well as on boats or on foot in his constant travels. The Paul who wrote Galatians 3:28 and Colossians 3:11 about unity in Christ is transparent in today's inclusion of so many co-workers. Who he was, was who they got. He was a walking, talking apostle-pastor-teacher-preacher. His heart and mind were captured by Jesus Christ, and everywhere he went he wanted to spread good news about Jesus. Jesus was, in fact, his good news. Paul was transparent. He wore his feelings on his sleeves and face. He told people what he thought. He expressed himself. When he was sad, he said so. When he was joyous, his face showed it. He was not the stereotypical glad-handing salesman. He was a genuine follower of Jesus, a genuine missionary, a genuine pastor, and a genuine human being. He was, in other words, transparent. There wasn't a private Paul and a platform Paul. The Paul behind the rostrum teaching was the Paul at dinner. Today we reflect on growing in transparency.

Transparent in Prayer

He encourages people to persist in wakeful praying and thanking God (4:2), and then asks them to pray for himself. But what he wants for himself, though he is "in chains," is "that God may open a door for our message," that is, "so that we may proclaim the mystery," and that mystery is Jesus Christ himself (4:3). He wants to make that mystery crystal-clear (4:4). It can't be done without the power of God at work. Dennis Edwards reminds that "conversation with God is prelude to conversations . . . with those outside the community of faith" (D. Edwards, "Colossians," 498).

When we ask people to pray for us, we can learn from Paul to pray that what God has called us to do, *regardless of our personal circumstances,* to use us for his glory. We all have stuff going on, and there is no reason to minimize our stuff. At times, our stuff gets in the way of what we are called to do. Paul had that experience (2 Corinthians 2:12–13), and Paul went through the wringer in ministry (2 Corinthians 11:21–33). But while locked down in chains, what he wanted most was for an opportunity to tell others about Jesus (cf. Acts 28:16–31). Some of our best ministry experiences can be in the midst of lots of stuff in our lives. Stuff reduces us to a desperate trust that makes us more transparent than we might otherwise be.

Transparent in Wisdom

What Paul had learned in about three decades of constant to-and-froing with the gospel (1) to "walk around in wisdom toward those outside" and, in wise-walking one learns what "purchasing the season" means, which the NIV translates as "make the most of every opportunity" (4:5; *Second Testament*).

What Paul expresses here is not manipulation of others, but the power of wise-walking to turn every moment into doing something "in the name of the Lord Jesus" (3:17). Faith has the power to reshape our words and deeds, especially in the public square. Ryan Burge, an American sociologist of Christianity, however, has detailed a powerful negative shift for church people. More and more people are choosing their church (and their faith) on the basis of their politics, rather than their politics on the basis of their faith. He concluded:

> People are picking their religion based on their politics, not their politics based on their religion. That means that moderates and liberals are feeling less and less welcome in evangelical churches and are heading to the exits, never to return.
>
> That also means that more and more Americans are being drawn to evangelicalism because of the political and cultural connotations of the term, with little regard for the theology. (Burge, "Did the Election . . .")

When what we believe does not effect how we live, we are in trouble. When what we believe most in is the power of politicians and politics, we are even more in trouble. Paul was reshaping his own life and the lives of others to live the whole of life under the aegis of Christ himself.

Paul had learned, in years of responding to anyone and everyone, to speak with others "in grace," even if we think he may have a generous definition of grace for some of his words or he may have some regrets about some of his polemical, heated comments, like those to Peter (Galatians 2:11–14) or like his angry words to the Corinthians (2 Corinthians 10–13). Failure can be a powerful teacher. He was transparent, then, in what he learned about how to communicate with others. One of his expressions was to put salt on the words. This is a "trope capable of various connotations and, as an analogy, creates the ambiguity and enlightenment that comes with an image" (McKnight, *Colossians*, 380). Go ahead, he was saying to the Colossians, explore how salt turns our words into grace. We are learning from his trope when we think of speaking wisely, graciously, intelligently, and redemptively. Because salt was at times connected to wittiness, some think he wants them to be charming and clever in their communication with outsiders. It was said of Stephen, when he was on the threshold of being murdered, that his interrogators "could not stand up against the wisdom the Spirit gave him as he spoke" (Acts 6:10).

Transparent in Appreciation

This letter ends on notes of appreciation of the many co-workers who were presently providing support—material, spiritual, pastoral, interpersonal—to him while in prison. He names ten of them, mentions their ethnicity without wishing to wipe it away, and then attaches a note of appreciation and even admiration, starting with two people who may have had more to do with this letter than we might know:

Tychicus, who was his letter courier back to Colossae
(and then onto Laodicea)
Onesimus, the enslaved man who has information
about Paul if they need it

Three Jewish ("of the circumcision") co-workers, "who have become consolers for me" (4:11, *Second Testament*):

Aristarchus, who greets them
Mark, well-connected, they know about him, he wants
them to welcome him

Jesus Justus, who greets them

Now five more:

Epaphras, the founder of the church—a Christ-slave, greets them, and like Paul was "always contesting for you in the prayers that you may stand complete and fully assured in all God's will" (4:12; *Second Testament*). He was laboring for three churches: Colossae, Laodicea, Hierapolis.

Luke, the doctor and author of the Gospel of Luke and Acts

Demas, greets them

Nympha, a woman who was a church planter, a host for a church, or the lead pastor of the church in Laodicea (4:15).

Archippus, who may have led with Philemon or, alternatively, been Philemon's son, was to hear from Paul that he wanted him to "complete the ministry" the Spirit had given to him

I love this because it shows both how caring Paul was and how much he publicly affirmed those who worked alongside him. He was not the narcissist some make him out to be, gathering people around him and making sure the glory all went his way, and silencing, bad-mouthing, or pushing out those who did not center himself. Unlike Truman Capote, who refused to credit his childhood and early adulthood friend, Harper Lee, for her substantive contributions to his famous *In Cold Blood*. No, Paul was full of appreciation and admiration of others. He was transparent who was doing gospel work. Those are signs of a healthy person.

I have a special interest in Nympha because she is a woman and because she obviously was a leader in some way.

She is the only woman named here, which contrasts with many named women in Romans 16. That Nympha's name appears here along with other co-workers indicates she was a gospel agent in (probably) Laodicea. A turn occurred in the last generation that has increasingly restricted women gifted by God, and the restrictions grieve the Spirit. Heather Matthews is not alone in naming the restrictions she experienced in the church. One of the readers of a post at my Substack, a post written by Becky Castle Miller, commented on Heather Matthews' statement: "sexism restrained and directed my life decisions in unrecognized ways." To this, another Heather, Heather Hart, wrote, "How many women have been diverted in their attempt to follow God's good plan for them? Countless. We are as numerous as the stars." (Miller, "Sexism"). Paul's inclusion of Nympha in this list is his affirmation of her role as his co-worker in the gospel.

Transparent to the End

"I, Paul, write this greeting in my own hand." Like Dietrich Bonhoeffer's utterly unreadable handwriting, Paul's handwriting made it clear his skill was not actual writing. "Remember my chains." He began and ended on this note of transparency about his situation (4:3, 18).

"The grace be with you."

And also with you!

QUESTIONS FOR REFLECTION AND APPLICATION

1. What do you notice about Paul's pastoral nature in the closing of this letter?

2. Describe some ways you see Paul being transparent in his letters.

3. Which co-laborers of your own would you like to appreciate? List them and think of what you want to honor about them.

4. What can you learn from Paul's prayer requests to help shape the ways you ask others to pray for you?

5. What is your key takeaway from this study of Colossians?

FOR FURTHER READING

Ryan Burge, https://www.graphsaboutreligion.com/p
/did-the-election-of-donald-trump.

Becky Castle Miller, "Sexism: Naming the Problem,"
https://scotmcknight.substack.com/p/sexism
-naming-the-problem/comments. The comment
by Heather Hart on the quotation of Heather
Matthews can be found there. Heather Matthews'
book: *Confronting Sexism in the Church: How
We Got Here and What We Can Do About It*
(Downers Grove: IVP Academic, 2024).

Also Available in the
New Testament Everyday Series

Ⓗ HarperChristian Resources.com